Volume 2

History and Travel Stories

From an Endless Road Trip

www.etaoinpublishing.com

Lost In Michigan

Publisher: Etaoin Publishing
              Saginaw, MI
              www.EtaoinPublishing.com

Cover Design: Rick Ratell
              Cleaverleaf Design Services
              Midland, MI

Ordering Information:
Books may be ordered from www.LostinMichigan.net

Printed in the United States of America

ISBN 978-0-9994332-2-5
Category —Michigan History

Dedicated to my parents, who support me no matter what crazy idea I come up with.

Acknowledgments

Thank you so much to all the people who purchased my first book. Your support and kind comments made Volume 2 possible. I hope you enjoy reading it and will take it with you the next time you get "Lost in Michigan."

Thank you to Matt Schutt for reading my first draft, and helping me fix my many errors. I am sure he must have been wondering what my two brain cells were thinking when I formed some of the sentences that I used.

Introduction

Michigan is full of amazing places and incredible people. Since there are so many stories I have learned about in my travels, I needed to publish a second book to share them with you. I tried to pick stories that cover a broad range of subjects and history. The stories range from inspirational to tragic and really strange, but all of them occur in Michigan.

If you are wondering about the boat on the cover it is the *Joseph Medill*, a Chicago fire-boat that was sitting in a field in Escanaba. I say was because someone told me it was cut up and hauled away for scrap while I was in the process of writing this book. It would have been one of the locations featured, but I removed it since I did not want to send you to see something that does not exist anymore. The unfortunate thing about writing stories of old forgotten things is that they are demolished by the unforgiving forces of time. At publishing time all the locations are still intact but as the old saying goes, "The only constant is change."

The locations in this volume start at the bottom of the state and then work north. Each story is independent of one another. You can read them in any order you wish. I have done my best to give an address that you can use in a GPS to help you find each location. Some places have no address, so I have given a description of where they can be found. Most locations are on public property, but some may be privately owned. Whether they are public or private, they may not be open to visitors, or they may only be open at scheduled times. Most places can be seen from public roads. I don't trespass and I advise anyone against it. Please be respectful to the places you visit. I hope after reading this book you will take an interest in traveling the back roads of Michigan and see what you can find.

Contents

Chapter 1 Southern Lower Peninsula

Chapter 2 Central Lower Peninsula

Chapter 3 Northern Lower Peninsula

Chapter 4 Upper Peninsula

Chapter 1

Southern Lower Peninsula

Hamburg

 **Location:** 10585 Hamburg Road, Hamburg, MI 48139

I was heading north from Ann Arbor, and I did not feel like taking the expressway since it gets congested. For the most part, I have driven that stretch of I-23 enough times that it's now rather boring, so I drove north on some back roads in the countryside. The roads wound their way through the woods and around the small ponds and lakes in the area. I ended up in the small town of Hamburg. In the middle of town stands a beautiful old wooden church with a Gothic-style steeple. The church is St. Stevens and is one of the oldest Episcopal churches in Michigan. The parish was organized in 1844 with the church constructed shortly afterwards. Some of the funds to build the church came from Hamburg, Germany where immigrants to the area were from.

The town of Hamburg was founded in 1837 and you may have guessed that it was named after Hamburg, Germany and, if so, you guessed correctly. The name seems obvious given the immigrants would have named it after their home town. Strangely it was not the first or second potential option. Three German settlers, two with the last name

Messers and one with the last name of Grisson, purchased the land in 1835 and built a grist mill for milling grains and a hotel. As the settlement grew, nineteen men gathered together to name the town. I am not sure why but they did not include the original three Germans that started the town. The group of men came up with the names of Steuben and Knox but were equally split on making a decision so they decided to include the three men who started settling the area. It was the German immigrants who named the town Hamburg.

After naming the town, a township hall was constructed. The building stood for over 100 years and on a cold December day in 1954, John Moore, who took care of the hall, lit the oil burning stove to warm it up and it exploded. John Moore was severely burned and died from the explosion. A fire truck was sent from Brighton and broke down on the way to Hamburg. The townspeople were able to get the fire under control and later decided they needed their own fire department instead of relying on surrounding cities for help. Across from the graceful wooden church is a red fire station. Although the station is no longer used for fighting fires, it still stands proudly serving the community.

If you are in the area between Brighton and Ann Arbor take a drive through the small town of Hamburg. It's a beautiful little town nestled among the ponds and trees of southern Michigan.

Trip Tip: There are plenty of places nearby for nature lovers to explore, including Waterloo, Pickney and Brighton Recreation Areas. Along with Huron Meadows and Hudson Mills Metro Parks.

8th Precinct Castle

Location: 4150 Grand River Avenue
Detroit, Mi 48208

In my mind, Detroit has always been, and will always be, one of the great cities in the United States. In the past few decades it has been facing some challenges and declining in population. In the late 1800s it was a mecca of commerce and wealth. As the population of southeast Michigan grew, farms were converted into neighborhoods. Such was the case with the farm of William Woodbridge, northwest of Detroit. It was developed into an upper middle class neighborhood in 1885 for the affluent citizens of Detroit. By the 1900s the area needed a police station, and in this area of prosperity no ordinary building would do. It was decided that famed architect Louis Kamper would design a magnificent new building to house the police that protected the citizens in the Woodbridge neighborhood. Kamper designed a French Renaissance castle-like building and it was constructed between 1900 and 1901 for a cost of $46,000. The average annual income for Americans back then was about $430.

The building was constructed as two separate buildings connected with a walkway. The larger building housed the police department, and the smaller one, featuring an arched door facing the road was the carriage house. In the early 1900s the police used horses and wagons to patrol the city. In later years it was converted into a garage for the patrol cars. The police stopped using the station in 1954 and it became offices for the Detroit Police Youth Bureau and the Personnel Division. In 2013 the building was sold and converted into a residential living complex known as the Castle Lofts.

Michi-Fact: Louis Kamper designed several prominent buildings in Detroit, including the Book-Cadillac Hotel and the Hecker Castle on Woodward.

Allendale's Grand Rapids Fire Station

Location: 6610 Lake Michigan Drive, Allendale, MI 49401

West of Grand Rapids, past Grand Valley State University on a busy but sparsely populated stretch of road, I saw this ornate brick building. It has a steeple like a church, but two garage doors in the front, so I figured it must have been a fire house and the steeple was a hose tower for drying hoses. It definitely seemed out of place. It looked like an old fire house that

6

would have been in a large city. The interesting thing is that it actually once stood on the corner of Leonard and Monroe streets in Grand Rapids as Engine House No. 5. Built in 1880, the grand old fire station was constructed of pale yellow and red bricks, and housed horse-drawn steam pumpers, and the horses that pulled them. As the years went by, motorized fire engines replaced the horses, and the fire station got a coat of red paint. After serving the community for a hundred years, it was decided in 1980 that a new fire station was needed to accommodate the modern fire equipment.

The proud fire station was slated for demolition. Instead it was disassembled over the course of 10 weeks and re-assembled brick by brick at its new location in Allendale. The Construction took about five years and it included restoring the bricks back to their original creamy white and red color. The magnificent structure is the home of the Engine House No. 5 Museum.

Trip Tip: The museum exhibits include an antique fire engine and horse drawn carriages, along with a plethora of vintage fire fighting equipment. You can learn more about the museum at www.enginehouse5.com

Kalamazoo Water Tower

Location: 1210 Oakland Drive
Kalamazoo, MI 49008

Standing in the center of the Kalamazoo Regional Psychiatric Hospital is an ornate brick water tower that looks like something out of a fairy tale. It looks as if Rapunzel is going to drape her long, golden hair out one of the windows. The historic tower was constructed of brick in 1895. Detroit architect B. F. Stratton designed the tower to compliment the buildings of the hospital. Its medieval look stands out in comparison to the more modern looking building that surrounds the tower. Back when the structure was built, the facility, known as the Michigan Asylum for the Insane, was a sprawling complex with several buildings and two farms. The original buildings were of ornate Victorian era construction similar to the Traverse City State Hospital, originally known as the Northern Michigan Asylum.

Michigan Governor Epaphroditus Ransom from Kalamazoo, recommended the state build an institution for the treatment of mental patients. Construction of the Michigan Asylum for the Insane began in 1854, and the first building was completed in 1859. Before the asylum, mentally ill people were locked away in attics, cellars or jail cells. The new hospital was a way for people to get treatment and a place to live. By 1959 the facility had grown into a small city with 3500 patients, and 900 staff members to provide care for them. It had its own power generating installation and water treatment plant.

By the 1970s other forms of treatments were available for mental health patients, and the population of the hospital declined. By the 80s funding for the facility had diminished and demolition of the buildings began. Some of the remaining buildings are still used for patients and some of the other buildings are utilized by Western Michigan University for its medical education programs.

As with any large psychiatric facility there are stories that make you wonder if it is haunted. A doctor was stabbed to death by a patient in 1904, and a nurse was strangled to death when a patient lured her into the basement in 1954. I am not sure if there are any spirits still residing in the hospital, but I am sure that old water tower has witnessed many things over the years.

The current hospital surrounds the tower that stands in its courtyard and is not accessible to the public. You can still see the top of the ornate tower standing tall over the hospital. It was slated for demolition by the state in 1974 but a group of citizens raised over $200,000 to restore the historic landmark.

Michi-Fact: In 1909, during the Burdick House hotel fire in Kalamazoo, firefighters lost water pressure and the water from the tower at the hospital was hooked up to the city water main to increase the pressure, saving downtown Kalamazoo.

Huron Lightship

Location: 800 Prospect Place
Port Huron, MI 48060

As sailors began transporting goods around the Great Lakes, lighthouses were built on the shoreline to guide captains away from danger. But some hazards to navigation, such as shoals and sandbars, are out in the middle of the lake. To warn passing ships of the danger. Lightships were constructed with a light on top of a mast and anchored near the hazard.

About six miles north of Port Huron is the Corsica Shoals, a hazard to ships sailing out of the St Mary's River into Lake Huron. Three lightships were anchored at the Shoal, and the final ship to advise captains of the danger under the water was the *Huron*. The proud lightship was built in 1921 and began its life as a relief vessel for other lightships. A crew of eleven sailed the ninety-seven foot long steel ship. In 1935, she was stationed at Corsica Shoals after serving in northern Lake Michigan. Only five years after anchoring off Corsica Shoals the other lightships were decommissioned leaving the *Huron* as the last remaining lightship on the Great Lakes. She proudly carried out her duties in the Coast Guard for another 30 years before being replaced by illuminated buoys in 1970. She was given to the city of Port Huron and permanently moored in sand, next to the St Mary's River. She's spending the rest of her retirement as a museum ship, reminiscing of the days illuminating the darkness in Lake Huron.

Michi-Fact: In 1832, the first lightship on the Great Lakes was placed at Waugoshance Shoal in the Straits of Mackinac. The wooden lightship *Lois McLain* was stationed at the shoal until 1851, when it was replaced by the Waugoshance Light.

Lansing 's Grand Trunk Railroad Station

Location: 1203 South Washington Avenue, Lansing, MI 48910

Before the automobile was invented, and Detroit became the Motor City, the quickest and easiest way to travel around the state of Michigan was by train. By the early 1900s almost every town had a train station, usually in the heart of the town. Passengers would get on or off the Pullman cars and goods were unloaded from box cars. Over time, as expressways were built, Michiganians began traveling by car instead of by rail. The once popular train station began seeing less passengers, and many stations were eventually abandoned and forgotten.

One such forgotten station that got a new life was the Grand Trunk Western Railroad Station in Lansing. The station was built in 1902, with a square tower that has battlements along the top to give it a castle-like look. Over the years the station has seen families take a trip for a summer vacation. Soldiers heading off and returning from war. Being in Lansing, I am sure it has seen its fair share of politicians heading off to the Capitol building to fulfill or break campaign promises.

In 1941 the station was rocked by tragedy, when a passing freight train carrying fruit from Chicago to Toronto derailed. It was traveling about fifty miles per hour when twenty-nine rail cars jumped the tracks, smashing into the train station and demolishing the western side of the station. Thirteen-year-old James Smith was selling magazines on the platform of the station and was killed by a refrigeration car. Twelve other people were injured. Firemen and police officers dug through the rubble of the station for four hours looking for other victims, but did not find anyone else caught up in the disaster.

By 1972 passenger trains no longer frequented the station with the square tower, and it was turned into a restaurant. It must have been a popular restaurant, since Michigan native and President Gerald R. Ford stopped for dinner while campaigning in 1976. Eventually the restaurant closed, and the once popular and grand old station sat vacant and abandoned.

In 2010 the Lansing Board of Water and Light built a new power plant next to the boarded up railroad station. They could have made the decision to knock it down and use the property for parking. Instead they decided to renovate the old station back to its former glory, and now use it for business meetings and community events.

Trip Tip: Another depot to see in Lansing is the Union Depot located at 637 E. Michigan Ave.

Belle Isle Aquarium

Location: 900 Inselruhe Avenue
Detroit, MI 48207

Belle Isle, in the Detroit River, is the largest city owned park in the country. Once Detroit was struggling financially, it was not able to maintain the island and leased it to Michigan. It is now part of the State Park system. Over a hundred years ago, Detroit was a mecca of manufacturing and the city hired famed architect Alber Kahn to design an aquarium. The ornate buildingm with its one of a kind carved stone entrance, opened in 1904 making it the oldest operating Aquarium in the United States.

For years it had been a popular destination for Detroiters, but during Prohibition its popularity grew with a secret speakeasy in the basement. With Canada on the other side of the Detroit River, where the manufacturing of alcohol was still legal, bootleggers "imported" many bottles of the valuable liquid into the United States. They would use boats in the summertime and drive across the ice on the frozen river during the winter months. The aquarium was a quick stop with a door on the side that led to the basement. With a secret knock, you could get inside to sell booze, if you made it across the river without getting stopped by the feds. There is also a story that a mermaid was kept in a bathtub at the secret night club, but that sounds more like someone dressed up to entertain the men. Or maybe they were enjoying the liquor a little too much and their brain on alcohol imagined the whole thing.

Since Belle Isle is now part of the state park system you will need to purchase a day pass to enter it, unless you have purchased a recreation passport for your Michigan license plate. Once you're on the island, admission to the aquarium is free and open on the weekends. This may change after this book is published, so be sure to check for more information at www.belleisleconservancy.org

Trip Tip: When visiting the aquarium you can also visit the Anna Scripps Whitcomb Conservatory, which is located next to the aquarium.

House of David

Location: 1055 E Britain Avenue, Benton Harbor, MI 49022

Near Benton Harbor is a massive palatial looking building. It was part of the Israelite House Of David, a religious commune that was founded by Benjamin and Mary Purnell in 1903. Benjamin Purnell was a traveling preacher from Kentucky, who one day declared himself the seventh and final messenger of God, as foretold in the Book of Revelation. He promised eternal life to all those who joined his commune. He believed they should be more like Jesus, and not cut their hair, including the men. The members of the commune stood out in Benton Harbor with their long hair flowing down to their waist, including the men. The members of the commune were prohibited from using alcohol, tobacco, eating meat, owning property, and were to remain celibate.

Despite these downsides, the House of David grew to hundreds of members by 1906, and they owned thousands of acres. They planted orchards and grew crops in their fields. They harvested enough fruit that they had their own cannery and operated a power plant to supply electricity. They were a self-sufficient group that had their own carpentry shop, tailor shop and laundry.

To occupy their time when they were not out working in the farm fields or doing chores, they played music and sports. The members played a lot of baseball and they excelled at the sport. The House of David baseball team began traveling the country playing teams in exhibition matches, defeating some of the best teams in the country. They were never allowed into the major league because of a rule banning facial hair. Their musicians traveled the country playing music to audiences in the vaudeville circuit.

The commune built an amusement park called Eden Springs which was known for its miniature train. The House of David opened their park up to the community and it became very popular. Many people traveled for miles to visit it. By 1916 the commune had more than a thousand members and attracted over half a million visitors to their amusement park.

The group became rather wealthy and well liked by the public until the 1920s, when thirteen young women confessed to having intercourse with the group's leader Benjamin Purnell when they were minors. After a lengthy and public trial, he was not convicted of having relations with minors, but he was convicted of fraud. Purnell died in 1927 before he was sentenced. The accusations caused the commune to split with Benjamin's wife Mary Purnell, taking half its members and creating a new commune down the street known as Mary's City of David. Over time the membership declined in both communes and the amusement park closed. Today there are a few members left. The Eden Springs Park has reopened, restoring one of the trains. The park is not what it used to be, but the train still gives rides to passengers.

Trip Tip: Down the street from the House of David is Mary's City of David, the commune started by Mary Purnell.

St Andrews Cathedral

Location: 301 Sheldon Avenue SE, Grand Rapids, MI 49503

I was roaming around downtown Grand Rapids with no particular destination in mind. I turned down a street to see a magnificent Gothic style church with steeples that reached up into the heavens. St. Andrews Cathedral was constructed in 1875 and in 1883 the Grand Rapids Diocese's first bishop, Henry J. Richter, consecrated the Cathedral.

During a Sunday evening service in 1901, lightning struck the cathedral at 9:30 P.M. and initially it was thought that no harm was done. However a smoldering fire had started in the roof, and by 2:19 A.M. the church was fully engulfed in flames. The roof and everything inside was destroyed by the fire but the brick walls remained standing. After the fire, the cathedral was reconstructed. Hidden above the ceiling are some of the charred wooden beams that survived the fire.

The church may have been built in 1875, but the parish traces its history all the way back to missionary priest Father Frederic Baraga. He built a small church, rectory and school on the west bank of the Grand River to minister to the Native Americans before moving to northern Michigan. A statue of Father Baraga stands in front of the cathedral commemorating his achievements.

Michi-Fact: In the mid 1960s, the cathedral was one of the first churches in the country to televise Sunday-morning mass live. A television studio was created in the church to broadcast around Grand Rapids.

Detroit's Masonic Temple

Location: 500 Temple Street, Detroit, MI 48201

    The Detroit Masonic Temple was designed by famed architect George Mason, who also designed the Grand Hotel on Mackinac Island with his partner Zachariah Rice. The cornerstone of the temple was placed on September 19, 1922, using the same trowel that George Washington had used to set the cornerstone of the United

States Capitol in Washington D.C. The building was dedicated on Thanksgiving Day, 1926.

There is a myth that architect George Mason went broke funding the construction and his wife left him, so he climbed to the top of the building and jumped off, but that is not true. He lived to be 92 years old and died in 1948. The building has over a thousand rooms, as well as several secret staircases, concealed passages, and hidden compartments in the floors. Strange things are said to happen, but I just think the old temple has a haunting beauty to it.

The Detroit Masonic Temple has been the largest Masonic Temple in the world since 1939, when the Chicago Masonic Temple was demolished. The stage of the auditorium is the second largest in the United States. The building houses two ballrooms: the Crystal Ballroom and the Fountain Ballroom, which accommodates up to a thousand people. There is also an unfinished theater located in the top floor of the tower that would have seated about seven hundred people. Several movies have been filmed on location at the temple including *Batman vs Superman* (there's three hours of my life I will never get back). The 17,500-square-foot drill hall has a floating floor, where the entire floor is laid on felt cushions. This type of construction, also known as a sprung floor, provides "give" to the floor, which tends to relieve the marchers.

In April 2013, the building was reported to be in foreclosure, with over $152,000 in back taxes owed to Wayne County. The debt was paid off by singer-songwriter Jack White, a Detroit native known for his work with The White Stripes. He wanted to help the temple as they had helped his mother in a time of need. The temple gave her a job as an usher in the theater when she was struggling to find work. In response, the Detroit Masonic Temple Association renamed its Scottish Rite cathedral the Jack White Theater.

Trip Tip: George Mason also designed the Ransom Gillis House, which was renovated by Nicole Curtis on the HGTV *Rehab Addict* show. The house is not far from the Masonic Temple in Brush Park, at 205 Alfred Street.

Holmdene Estate

Location: 1700 Fulton Street East, Grand Rapids, MI 49506

Holmdene Hall, on the campus of Aquinas College in Grand Rapids, started out as the home of the Lowe family. Edward Lowe and his wife Susan came from wealthy families and when Susan's father Delos A. Blodgett retired from his lumbering business he gave one third of his fortune to his daughter. Susan and Edward then purchased a 69-acre dairy farm on the outskirts of Grand Rapid. In 1908 construction was completed of their magnificent home, built in the Tudor style of Europe. They named their new home Holmdene Manor, after "holm" which is a particular type of oak tree and "dene" which means "estate". The Lowes were such prominent members of Grand Rapids society that President Theodore Roosevelt stayed in their home when he visited Grand Rapids for a speech in 1911.

While Edward and Susan Lowe raised their family in their ornate European style mansion and gardens, a group of Dominican nuns came to the city to start a school. The Sisters came to Grand Rapids in 1887, after starting a school in Traverse City. In 1910, they established the Novitiate Normal School and by 1923 the school evolved into a college for women. They received a charter from the state of Michigan to grant degrees. The college continued to thrive in downtown Grand Rapids, and in 1931 it became the first Catholic Junior College to teach both men and women. As the college continued to grow it became a four year institution in 1940, and was renamed Aquinas College in honor of St. Thomas Aquinas.

As the Dominican Sisters continued to educate at Aquinas College, the Lowes lived in their home outside of Grand Rapids. Susan Lowe died resting in her garden in 1931, at the age of 58. Edward Lowe lived at Holmdene without his wife, until he died in 1938. The expansive estate was sold to the University of Grand Rapids. The university only used the property for a few years until it closed. In 1945, the now expanding Aquinas Collage purchased the Holmdene Manor and estate, which was built on the old dairy farm. Over the years the college built new buildings on the grounds and it is now a beautiful campus in Grand Rapids. The historic mansion is still used by the college as offices for the administration.

Holmdene is a grand old home with a long history and like some other historic places, stories of strange happenings began to surface. Students and staff have reported lights mysteriously turning on and off. The elevator seems to be operating as if someone was in it, even when there is no one inside. Others say doors slam shut on their own. Some of the hauntings are perpetuated by a myth that Mr Lowe's son James drowned in a pond on the property, or that he fell down a dumbwaiter shaft and died, but that is not true. He moved to San Francisco and became a successful businessman, and died at the age of 65. Haunted or not, Holmdene is a spectacular home and it's wonderful that it is still being maintained and used by Aquinas College.

Trip Tip: A few miles west of Aquinas College on Fulton Street is the heart of the Heritage Hill Historic District. It's one of the largest historic districts in the United States and, driving around the neighborhood, you can see some of the most spectacular homes in Grand Rapids.

The Castle of Oz

Location: 6700 Bryant Avenue
Castle Park, Holland, Michigan 49473

Standing near the shoreline of Lake Michigan, south of Holland, is an old brick castle with a story almost like a fairy tale. The castle was built in 1876 by German immigrant and Chicago businessman, Michael Schwarz. His family of six daughters and two sons, lived in the castle for about a year. Being isolated from civilization was something the girls who grew up in Chicago could not adapt to and missed the big city life the once had. The family moved to Holland and left the castle abandoned.

Reverend John Parr, who founded the Chicago Preparatory School was visiting the area, when he noticed the abandoned castle and fell in love with it. He purchased the Castle in 1893, turning it into a summertime camp for the boys and girls of Chicago. Rev. Parr and his wife ran the camp and it became so popular that he sold his school to run the camp full time in 1896. When the parents of the campers came to visit their children, they marveled at the natural beauty of the Lake Michigan shoreline. Seizing on a opportunity, the reverend and his wife converted the castle into an inn and resort. The Industrial Revolution created a wealthy class of Americans who could afford to travel, and the popularity of the resort grew. Chicago's and Milwaukee's wealthiest families could take a passenger steamer across Lake Michigan to the dock in Macatawa, where it was a short carriage ride to Castle Park. After expanding the castle and inn to meet demand, Parr began selling small lots for guests to build cottages and become part of the "Castle Club." In 1917, Reverend Parr's nephew, Carter Brown and his wife took over the duties of running the resort. By 1960, the camp had grown tremendously, taxes and maintenance had become too much to handle so the camp became Castle Park, a private association. The association owns the magnificent castle and it is used as a library and meeting place.

Every great castle has a legend and this yellowish brick palace is no exception. One of the most well known visitors to Castle Park was author L. Frank Baum, who wrote the beloved book, *The Wizard of Oz*. He had a summer cottage nearby in Macatawa. It is said that the castle partly inspired his tale of Dorothy and her dog Toto, and that some of the residents of Castle Park were his inspiration for a few of the characters. Exactly how much the castle inspired Baum is unknown, but he frequently traveled to western Michigan to relax and get away from the pressures of daily life. Roger S. Baum, the great-grandson of L. Frank Baum stated, "Most people don't realize that *The Wizard of Oz* was written in Chicago, and the Yellow Brick Road was named after winding cobblestone roads in Holland, Michigan, where great-grandfather spent vacations with his family." I can imagine Baum traveling from his cottage in Macatawa to Castle Park. It must have been like another world, with its castle dominating the lakeside community and would resemble Dorothy's journey to the Emerald City.

Castle Park remains as a private community.

Peninsular Paper Company

Location: 1249 Leforge Road, Ypsilanti, MI 48198

The Huron River winds its way through southeast Michigan over several dams, generating electricity, until it reaches Lake Erie and the mouth of the Detroit River. The mighty river flows near the town of Ypsilanti, and north of Eastern Michigan campus there is a dam where the waters of the Huron River flow over it. At the north end of the dam is an old abandoned building with a giant sign on top that reads PENINSULAR

PAPER CO. The old building is the remains of a powerhouse used to generate electricity for the Peninsular Paper Company. The plant was constructed in 1867, to supply the *Chicago Tribune* with paper for printing. I thought it seemed strange that they would get paper from a town so far away from Chicago. I found out that they already had one supplier, but wanted another one far from the first one in case there was ever a fire at one of the plants. They wanted to ensure that it would not interrupt their supply of paper. Sadly, in 1873, the Peninsular Papermill caught fire and burned down and the *Chicago Tribune* canceled their contract. Peninsular Paper still had enough customers to build a new mill, and continued operating it on the Huron River until 2001. The old paper mill on the south end of the dam was demolished and apartment complexes were built in its place. The six acres of property on the north end of the dam was purchased by the city of Ypsilanti and is now Peninsular Park. The empty powerhouse stands on park property and is accessible for some urban exploration. If you want to check out an old dam building, and you're near Ypsilanti, stop by Peninsular Park.

War Dog Memorial

Location: 25805 Milford Road
South Lyon, MI 48178

For years trees and shrubs grew on a wooded lot at the corner of Milford Road and 11 Mile near South Lyon. Cars drove past it for years paying little attention to this little piece of land. It was not until 2010 that it was discovered to be a pet cemetery and in the middle of it was a giant stone monument memorializing the war dog. Hundreds of volunteers cleaned up the old forgotten cemetery and it currently is the Michigan War Dog Memorial. The site was originally set up by the Elkow family in 1936 and known as the Happy Hunting Grounds Pet Cemetery. In 1946, when news of how many lives had been saved by War Dogs during WWII, local residents raised money to install a monument to show their respect to the heroic K-9s. Present at the dedication of the sixteen ton granite monument was a doberman pinscher named Sargent Sparks, a Marine Corps scout and messenger dog that carried messages and medical supplies at Guadalcanal and Okinawa. A year after the dedication, someone poisoned Sgt. Sparks near his Rochester home. His master requested that he be buried wrapped only in a blanket, like so many of his buddies at the beaches. He was laid to rest at the base of the monument.

One of the most famous dogs buried at the cemetery is Blizzard, one of Admiral Byrd's lead sled dogs. He was at the Chicago Worlds Fair and was sold to people who lived in Windsor. When Blizzard died in 1937 at 12 years of age, he was buried at the cemetery. Along with Blizzard is a parrot that was on Admiral Dewey's flagship. The colorful bird was owned by the city of Detroit when it died at 86 years. (Parrots can live to be 150 years old!)

If a military working dog is killed in action or dies while on active duty at their home base, they are buried with honors by the military. If a military working dog is adopted out and dies, the Michigan War Dog Memorial and Cemetery is a place for a heroic K-9 to be laid to rest at no cost to the owner. There have been several dogs who served from all

U.S. wars since 1936 that have been laid to rest along with police K-9s and other loyal working dogs.

Trip Tip: If you visit the memorial be sure to park on 11 Mile Road since Milford road has a lot of fast moving traffic, and there is also a ditch next to the road.

Chapter 2
Central Lower Peninsula

Minnie Quay's Tragic Tale

 **Location:** Lake Huron Shoreline Forester, MI on M-25 a few miles north of M-46

It's hard to imagine that Michigan's Thumb was once covered in a thick dense forest. It is mostly farmland today because the lumberjacks harvested most of the timber. Many ships tied up to the docks at Forester to fill their cargo holds full of lumber. Fifteen-year-old Minnie Quay met a young man who worked on one of those ships and fell madly in love with him. Minnie's family owned a tavern in Forester and her mother did not approve of Minnie's relationship with a sailor. Townspeople have said that her mother told Minnie she would rather see her dead than marry a sailor. Her mother would not allow Minnie to see the man she loved, and she never said goodbye to him the last time his ship left Forester.

A few days later word came back to Forester that the ship had sank in a storm on the Great Lakes and all the crewmen drowned. Minnie was devastated upon hearing the news of her lovers death . About a week after on April 27, 1876, her parents had to go on a trip, and left Minnie at home to watch her infant brother. While her brother lay sleeping, she put on her white dress and walked out of her house. Passing the Tanner Inn, she waved to the people on the porch who said hello. She continued walking to the end of the dock that stretched out into Lake Huron. The people at the Tanner Inn watched in horror when she jumped into the frigid water without hesitation. An hour later her lifeless body was pulled from the freezing cold water by men with grappling hooks.

She was laid to rest in the Forester Township Cemetery along Lake Huron north of town. Many people say that they have seen a young woman in white roaming the beaches. It's believed to be Minnie's spirit waiting for her sailor to return back to Forester.

Michi-fact: The building the Tanner Inn occupied is still standing in Forester today. During Prohibition it was used as a speakeasy.

House of Gould

 **Location:** 515 North Washington Street, Owosso, MI 48867

North of downtown Owosso, on Washington Street, is an Italianate creamy yellow brick mansion that is hard to miss. It was built for Amos Gould in 1860. After moving to Owosso from New York, he was elected as the city's first mayor. He also organized the first bank in Owosso, operating it out of this house. Amos and his brother Ebenezer opened a law firm together. After the attack of Fort Sumter they both wanted to serve in the military, so they decided to flip a coin. One would join the military and the other would stay to run the law practice and care for both families. Amos lost the coin toss. Ebenezer returned home from the Civil War a hero, he had risen to the rank of Colonel and had been wounded in battle at Hagerstown, Maryland.

After the Civil War, the demand for lumber grew, and Amos purchased large tracts of land in the Upper Peninsula. The town of Gould City was named after him in 1886. Amos also organized the Michigan Central Railroad when it was extended from Jackson to Saginaw. In 1852, he was elected to the Michigan State Senate. After serving in Lansing, he retired from public life and lived in his home until his death in 1882. The house is now owned by the Owosso Historical Commission, where it is used for special events and tours by appointment.

Trip Tip: Besides the Gould House, there are several other beautiful old ornate houses in Owosso. I love driving around the area near Oliver Street and looking at them.

Stepping Stone Falls

Location: 5161 Branch Road, Flint, MI 48506

There are several dams around Michigan, but the dam on the Flint River that created C.S. Mott Lake is unique. One end of the dam has concrete columns and steps for the water to cascade over, creating the Stepping Stone Falls. Charles Stewart Mott was an engineer and an executive at General Motors. He was also on the board of General Motors for sixty years from 1913 until his death in 1973.

C.S. Mott was generous with the money he had made in the automobile industry, helping Flint pave roads and build a modern sewer system. In his later years he wanted to build an area north of Flint for people to enjoy nature. In 1971 the C.S. Mott Foundation funded a dam that created the 650 acre C.S. Mott lake in the Genesee Recreation Area. It also includes the area encompassing the Huckleberry Railroad and Crossroads Village.

Michigan has several waterfalls, but many of them are in the Upper Peninsula. If you are like me and love taking photos of waterfalls, you will enjoy a visit to the Stepping Stone Falls. Even though they are man-made they are beautiful to watch. The water cascades down around the columns and along the steps.

Michi-Fact: The name of the falls were determined by a contest, and the name Stepping Stone Falls by Debbie Holbrook of Flint, was chosen as the winner in 1972.

Linden Mills

Location: 201 North Main Street
Linden, Michigan 48451

I was driving around exploring the southern part of the
Mitten State west of Fenton, when I came upon a
picturesque colonial-looking mill on the Shiawassee River in
Linden. The charming historic village was settled by
brothers Richard and Perry Lamb in 1835 and given the
name Linden, after the tree of the same name. The

brothers provided housing to weary travelers headed across Michigan. In 1845, Seth Sadler and Samuel W. Warren built the current mill standing in the heart of town. The mill housed both a gristmill and a sawmill. A gristmill is a building that grinds grain into flour, whether it is corn, wheat or any other kind of grain. The mill continued grinding grain into flour for over a century, until it shut down in 1956 and the machinery was sold at auction. The former mill was purchased by the city, and used as an office. Part of the building was also converted into a public library. Recently a portion of the mill has been renovated, and turned into a museum displaying artifacts from the region.

Trip Tip: The Shiawassee Heritage River Water Trail flows through the city of Linden. The trail is eighty-eight miles long and goes from Holly to Chesaning. https://www.shiawasseewatertrail.org/

Garfield Inn

Location: 8544 Lake St, Port Austin, MI 48467

Known as the Garfield Inn, the grand old Second Empire home in Port Austin was built by Charles G. Learned. He was a native of New York and his father was a public works contractor. At the age of eighteen, and relying on his father's reputation he received a contract to build a portion

48

of the aqueduct carrying fresh water to the city of New York. He earned ten thousand dollars in 1835 from his contract, which was a rather large sum of money in its day, especially for a teenager. A few years later he married the love of his life, Maria Raymond and they lived on a small farm while the enterprising young Learned continued with his contracting business, working on projects in the north eastern states. Charles and Maria befriended a young college student by the name of James A. Garfield who would become the twentieth President of the United States. Garfield would live with the Learneds between semesters.

In the 1850s Charles Learned began investing in the Michigan lumbering business and by 1859 he had sold or leased his companies in New York and moved his family to Michigan. He purchased a modest home in Port Austin and over the years he built several additions to the house, creating the grand Second Empire mansion that stands today. When Garfield was a senator he would frequently visit the Learned's home. Only four months after Garfield became president, he was shot by an assassin's bullet and died seventy-nine days later. While in recovery from his wounds he said that he wished to go to Port Austin and stay with the Learneds, but he died before he ever had the chance.

Maria Learned died in 1881, and Charles joined her in the beyond ten years later in 1891. Their son Jonas Learned and his family continued to live in the house until 1931, when it was sold to a Mr. Mayes who renamed the home the Mayes Inn, and operated it as a tourist home, bar, and restaurant. In 1946 it was purchased by a Mr. Neinaltowski, who changed the name to the Tower Hotel. In 1989 it was purchased by the Pasant Family and renamed the Garfield Inn. It was recently sold to new owners who have been renovating the old mansion into one of the top Bed and Breakfasts in the state. The dining room is also open for dinner on Friday and Saturday evenings. You can find out more at www.thegarfieldinn.com

Michi-Fact: Charles' only son Jonas ran a mercantile business in the nearby town of Port Crescent. The remains of the town can be seen at Port Crescent State Park near Port Austin.

Ammi Wright House

Location: 503 North State Street
Alma, MI 48801

Alma is located in the center of the Lower Peninsula and standing in the heart of Alma is an old stone Richardsonian-design house. Built in 1888 by lumber baron and business man Ammi Wright, the house was advanced for its time with its own hot water system. The Wright

51

family owned the house until it was sold in 1934 and converted into Smith Memorial Hospital. For years the old building served the community treating patients, and over three thousand babies were born in its rooms. As medicine advanced, the hospital outgrew the old house and in 1959 Northwood Institute moved in, using the rooms to educate students. Eventually the college moved to its current location in Midland. After a few other businesses used the old mansion it was left empty. A new owner has plans to renovate the old house and convert it into a European style hotel.

Michi-Fact: Besides the house being the start of Northwood University, the home's original owner, Ammi Wright, donated land in Alma, and built two buildings to help create Alma College.

Wahjamega

Location: M-81 and South Graf Road across from the airport west of Caro

If you are traveling in the Thumb on M-81 west of Caro, you may see a strange complex of buildings. They look out of place in Michigan with the tan stucco exterior and dark reddish brown tile roofs. When I saw them for the first time they looked like they were part of an elaborate resort, but the truth is far more interesting. I always thought it was a Native American name, but the name Wahjamega is an acronym from the initials of three partners who operated a sawmill here: William A Heartt, James A. Montgomery, and Edgar George Avery. They started the mill in 1852, and by 1853 the town was large enough that it was granted a post office. William A. Heartt was the first postmaster. By 1905 the lumber boom was over. The town's population declined and the post office was closed.

In 1914, The Farm Colony for Epileptics was established in Wahjamega by the state, and was devoted to the treatment of epilepsy. Much of the original population of the facility was moved from the overcrowded Lapeer State Home for Epileptics. The site was chosen for its rich soil and access to the railroad. The colony grew to include six houses, a hotel building, a store, barns and a blacksmith shop. There were several other small buildings such as a milk house, an ice house, and a chicken house. The farm also included a 40-acre apple tree orchard. By 1925, the colony had a population of 800 people. In 1937, the name was changed to the Caro State Hospital for Epileptics and farming operations ceased in 1950. The population of the hospital continued to grow and at its peak in 1967 there were 1800 people living and working at the facility.The population began its decline as the state of Michigan changed its laws and how it cared for mentally ill residents. Over time the buildings became dilapidated and many are no longer used.

The main building houses the Caro Center, a mental health facility run by the state and is Tuscola County's second largest employer.

Michi-Fact: In 1923, Michigan passed a eugenics law requiring the sterilization of feeble-minded and insane people. Over 3700 people in Michigan institutions were sterilized by surgery or x-rays. Both men and women were forced to have the procedure as recently as 1963.

Ithaca Fire Station and Monument

Location: 129 West Emerson Street, Ithaca, MI 48847

Standing in the beautiful town of Ithaca is a historic brick fire station. You may notice the custom-made weather vane with a metal firefighter climbing a ladder. Next to the fire station, you may notice the stone memorial but you probably have never heard of the man that it memorializes.

After graduating from the University of Michigan in 1874, Henry R. Pattengill became the superintendent of schools for the rural community of St. Louis in central Michigan. He then became the superintendent of Ithaca Schools and later president of the Gratiot County Teachers Association. He was passionate about rural children receiving a good education and helped create many schools and libraries in the farming towns of Michigan. Pattengill rose to the level of Michigan's Superintendent of Public Instruction in 1893. During his four years in office he created programs for free textbooks for students and certifications for teachers. To show support for his rural students when he visited city schools he would ask the children to raise their hands if they knew how to milk a cow or harvest wheat. He ran for Governor of Michigan in 1914, but lost the election. He died in 1918, leaving a legacy of educating all children in the state of Michigan, no matter where they lived. In 1924, his former students in Ithaca wanted to show their appreciation and built a monument in his honor. His former students donated 510 stones which came from twenty different states and twenty five Michigan counties.

It's strange that I was not able to find much information about Mr Pattengill. There are a lot of memorials to politicians and war heroes but not many to educators. If it were not for the stone monument that was built by his pupils, I would have never known about Henry R. Pattengill.

Michi-Fact: Ithaca was originally called Gratiot Center for its location in Gratiot County. It was renamed in 1857 after the town of the same name in New York.

Ovid's Gothic Church

Location: 222 N. Main St., Ovid, Michigan 48866

When traveling around the state I like to leave the main roads and explore the less traveled back roads. While out exploring the center of the Lower Peninsula I came across the town of Ovid. Standing near the center of town is a unique gothic-looking wooden church. The First Congregational Church in Ovid was built in 1872 on the corner of High and Park Streets. You may have noticed the current address is on Main Street. That's because the church was moved by a team of oxen in 1899 and additions were built onto the old church for the growing congregation. The church was listed on the National Register of Historic Places and in 1979 it was converted to a private residence.

Michi-fact: In the late 1800s Ovid was known for its carriage building factories and to celebrate their past they hold a "Carriage Days" festival is held every September.

Omer's Masonic Lodge

 **Location:** The corner of Center Road (M-23) and George Street in Omer, MI 48749

If you have ever traveled on M-23 along the Lake Huron shoreline you have probably driven past the stately two story building in Omer. After Arenac County was formed, Omer was chosen as the county seat. After the first courthouse burned down, a new one was built in its place in 1890. A year after the building was completed, at a cost of almost three-thousand dollars, instead a county-wide vote selected Standish as the county seat. The government moved to its new city instead of Omer. The vacant building was sold to the Freemasons for five hundred dollars and they used the grand old building as their lodge. Serving as the Omer Masonic Lodge for over a hundred years the building began to require a lot of maintenance and the Masons sold the building. A local couple purchased the historic building and did some much needed repairs to the foundation. The current owner is the Arenac County Historical Society, and they have been continuing the restoration efforts. The Historical Society uses the building for events and housing artifacts. It is open to the public for different fund-raising events. You can find out more at their website http://www.arenachistory.org/

Michi-fact: Omer proclaims itself to be Michigan's smallest city with a population of about 300 people. Technically Lake Angelus is Michigan's smallest city with a population of 290. Lake Angelus is a wealthy neighborhood that incorporated as a city to keep from being annexed. In my heart Omer will always be Michigan's smallest city.

Port Hope Chimney

Location: 8421 State Street, Port Hope, MI 48468

From a distance, this tall structure in Port Hope looks like a lighthouse since it's so close to Lake Huron, near the tip of the Thumb. After you get up close you realize it is something different. Thankfully there is a historical marker next to it that tells you what it is and its significance. The towering brick structure still standing in the middle of Stafford County Park, is all that remains of the sawmills that operated in Port Hope. It was constructed in 1858 by local mason John Geitz for lumberman William

R. Stafford, who built a sawmill on the site. He and his business partner William Southard purchased land from the federal government in the area for timber. The government had set aside the property for pensions for veterans of The War Of 1812. The sawmill and the town thrived with the booming lumbering business. In 1871, the Great Fire destroyed much of the town and sawmill but it was rebuilt and continued to operate. Ten years later, a second fire burned down the sawmill and most of the standing timber in the Thumb. Instead of rebuilding the sawmill, Stafford built a flour mill and a dock that stretched out into Lake Huron. The town continued to support the surrounding farmers as ships sailed into Port Hope to transport wheat and grain. Although the town has changed over the years, the brick chimney still stands as a reminder of the Thumbs lumbering past.

Michi-Fact: The town of Port Hope got its name when Stafford's partner William Southard first came to the area and was dropped off on a skiff a long ways from shore. As he rowed into the wind he said if they ever g0t to shore he was going to name it Port Hope.

Trip Tip: Point Aux Barques is seven miles north of Port Hope.

Shepherd Train Depot

Location: Corner of Wright and First Street in Shepherd, MI 48883

South of Mount Pleasant, on the Salt River, is the town of Shepherd. For a while it was known by two names. A flour mill and sawmill were built on the river in 1857. Using the power of the river to operate the mills, the little community was given a post office and known as Salt River. In 1885, the Ann Arbor Railroad laid down tracks west of the village and Isaac N. Shepherd build a depot for the train to stop in the small town. Many passengers disembarked at the Shepherd depot, and as the area around the train station grew it was known as Shepherd. In 1887 fire devastated many of the buildings near the Salt River. A new post office was built near the train depot to replace the one in Salt River. The new post office was given the name Shepherd and from then on that is what the town was known as. Although passenger service ended in the 1960s, the little depot still stands as a museum. If you visit it, there are several pieces of railroad history on display including an old diesel locomotive and an Ann Arbor Railroad caboose.

Trip Tip: The last full weekend of April is the Maple Syrup Festival in Shepherd.

Croton Dam

Location: 5380 Croton Drive
Newaygo, MI 49337

The Croton Dam has been holding back the flowing waters of the Muskegon River and generating electricity since 1906. At 110,000 volts, the plant generated the highest voltages at the time it was constructed. People traveled for miles by train to visit this extraordinary dam. They were given a tour of the powerhouse and treated to a dinner afterwards. Engineers from around the world, including Russia, England, France, Italy, Japan, and India, came to tour the dam and learn how to design better dams for their countries.

Some say the dam is haunted by the spirit of a young boy who was fishing from the top of the dam. It is said that he fell off the dam and into the turbines, killing him instantly. They say you can see his ghost walking along the top of the dam in the early morning hours. Local fishermen claim that whoever sees the apparition of the young boy first will have a prosperous day of fishing.

The Dam is near the historic little town of Newaygo and at the south end of the Huron-Manistee National Forest. It's well worth a trip not only to see the dam, but it is also an excellent location for fishing on the Muskegon River. Kimble County Park is near the foot of the dam and an excellent spot to launch a canoe or kayak.

Michi-Fact: The town of Croton was named after Croton, New York because of its similar terrain. It also has a dam as part of the New York Water System. The current dam's construction began in 1892 and was completed about the same time as the dam in Michigan.

White River Lighthouse

Location: 6199 Murray Road
Whitehall, MI 49461

William Robinson was appointed as the first keeper of the White River Lighthouse, located at the mouth of the White River, north of Muskegon. After it was built in 1875, keeper Robinson and his wife Sarah moved into the little brick lighthouse, where they raised their thirteen children. William Robinson was the head keeper for 47 years, at which time the Lighthouse Board decided that since he was 87 years old, the assistant keeper should take over the duties of maintaining the lighthouse. The assistant keeper was William Bush and he was Robinson's grandson. A few days before Bush officially took over the duties of running the lighthouse, his grandfather William peacefully died in the lighthouse that he loved and worked at for so many years. It is said that he and his wife's spirits still remain at the lighthouse, watching over it.

Michi-Fact: White River got its name from Native Americans who called it "Wabish-Sippe," meaning "the river with white clay in the water."

Saginaw's Castle

Location: 500 Federal Avenue
Saginaw, MI 48607

It's hard to believe that the magnificent castle that stands in the heart of downtown Saginaw faced demolition not once but twice. I can't imagine anyone wanting to destroy such a beautiful building. The building was built in 1898 by the United States Post Office. At the time they wanted to erect buildings that enhanced the community and reflected the surrounding area. The building's architect, William Martin Aiken, designed a European-Chateau style castle to honor the French fur traders that came to the Saginaw Valley. The original building was a square design with four turrets on each corner. By the 1930s the city of Saginaw's population grew with the prosperity of automobile manufacturing. This created a demand for mail and the grand post office was too small. The government decided to knock down the castle and build a new post office. The citizens of Saginaw protested and after a few years of deliberations with the government the decision was made to expand the castle. One of the turrets was removed and a large sorting room was added to the back of the castle.

By the 1960s, the castle was once again too small to handle all the mail that was passing through its stone walls. A new modern post office was built and the the castle was left empty. Since the structure was no longer being used once again the government proposed to raze the castle. For a second time, the citizens of Saginaw cried out to save their beloved castle. The Saginaw County Board of Commissioners placed the majestic and almost hundred year old structure on the National Register of Historic Places to help preserve it for future generations. It now serves as the home for the Historical Society of Saginaw and is a museum full of artifacts on display. If you are near Saginaw, I recommend stopping by the museum to check out the displays, but more importantly to walk the halls of this magnificent castle. You can even access the hidden hallway the postal inspectors used to "spy" on the employees sorting the mail from its days as a post office.

Trip Tip: The Mid-Michigan Children's Museum is about a mile away from the Castle Museum at 315 W. Genesee Avenue.

The Beer-Drinking Bear of Quanicassee

Location: Old State Road near the Quanicassee River 48733

Standing in a field on Old State Road, near the Quanicassee River, is a monument of a bear drinking from a bottle. If the monument could talk it would have an interesting yet sad story to tell. Frank Vanderbilt owned a hotel and resort in Quanicassee and as a way to attract visitors, he opened a small zoo. Sometime around 1910 he purchased a bear cub for his little zoo and named her

Jennie. He left her chained to a nearby tree stump and the visitors to his resort would feed her treats and candy.

One day someone gave her a bottle of beer and she gulped it right down like a thirsty lumberjack! Not long after that, Frank began selling beer to tourists to give to the little bear. She would climb up to the top of the tree stump,open the beer and drink it down. Her fame grew as word spread of the bear that enjoyed the frosty beverage and people came from all around Michigan to see Jennie. I wouldn't say life was good for Jennie, but she had her daily routine and the admiration of visitors.

Everything changed in 1920 when Prohibition became law and alcohol was illegal for Americans to own or sell, and that included Jennie. When she was no longer able to get beer, she became agitated and angry, growling at visitors and swiping her paws at Frank. They gave her bottles of soda pop and other beverages but she was not interested in them since she was addicted to alcohol. A group of men from Detroit were hunting in the Thumb and they stopped by the old hotel in Quanicassee. They told Mr. Vanderbilt that they would take care of the distraught bear and he sold Jennie to them. Later he found out that they used her for their hunting club's bear roast. Saddened by the loss of Jennie, Frank built this memorial to the bear with the money he received when he sold her.

Michi-Fact: The name Quanicassee is of Native American origin, meaning "lone tree."

Lost In Michigan

Chapter 3
Northern Lower Peninsula

Alabaster Loading Dock

Location: in Lake Huron south of Tawas

If you have ever traveled along US-23 south of Tawas, you have probably seen a ghostly building out in Lake Huron. It's all that remains of a loading dock for freighters to load cargo holds with gypsum. The town of Alabaster was named after a variety of gypsum discovered in the region by Douglass Houghton in 1837.

First used as fertilizer and then as an ingredient in plaster, gypsum is now used principally in the manufacturing of wallboard. B.F Smith opened a quarry near Alabaster in 1862 to mine the gypsum deposits. A fire in 1891 destroyed the operation but it was rebuilt in time to supply material for the main buildings at the Chicago Columbian Exposition of 1893, also known as the "World's Fair" where the Ferris Wheel was introduced. The exposition had ornate buildings, with marble-like walls earning it the title of "The White City," and greatly expanded gypsum sales.

In 1898, the company name was changed to the Alabaster Company. In 1902, the mine was incorporated into the U.S. Gypsum Corporation. The demand for gypsum soared as it was used in a variety of products including toothpaste, fertilizer, and plaster. It is the only natural substance that can be returned to a rock-like state with the addition of water, and is the main ingredient in Plaster of Paris. To meet demand and aid in the loading of ships, an elevated marine tramway was constructed in 1928 and stretched 1.3 miles out into the Saginaw Bay. Like a horizontal ski-lift, the cable system carried 72 "buckets" of gypsum to a waiting ship or to the storage bin in the loading building. Each bucket held more than two tons. The tramway included 6,450 feet of one and three-quarter inch steel cable and 14,000 feet of three-quarter inch cable. At a length of 6,350 feet, it was the longest over-water bucket tramway in the world. The tramway was demolished in the 1990s, but the loading building still remains offshore on Lake Huron south of Tawas.

Trip Tip: You can see the building from shore, but some binoculars or a telephoto lens for your camera will help you see it better.

Pere Cheney

Location: Center Plains Trail between Grayling and Roscommon

Before Grayling was the county seat of Crawford County, one of the largest towns in the area was Pere Cheney. It was a lumbering town established in 1874 by George Cheney who received a land grant from the Michigan Central Railroad. The population grew to about 1500 people and included a general store, railroad depot, post office, sawmill and hotel with telegraph service. Sadly, in 1893, diphtheria spread throughout the village, killing most of its citizens. In 1897, diphtheria returned and by 1917 there were only eighteen people left in the town, so it was sold off in an auction. Since then, all the buildings have disappeared, and only a cemetery remains, about a mile south of where the town once stood.

Because of the tragic demise of the town, rumors began to spread that it was built on an old Indian burial ground. Another rumor is that a witch cast a curse on the town after being banished into the nearby woods. There are reports of lights in the woods, and they say you can hear children playing, and sometimes they leave hand prints on the cars when you visit. Only a few headstones remain in the graveyard and many are broken or have fallen over. But that does not stop visitors from leaving flowers and coins.

Where the town once stood ,a lot of moss is growing on the trees. They say nothing grows there, but that's not true. There is wild grass growing and I even found some wildflowers. There are some depressions in the ground that mark where the buildings once stood.

The spooky thing about Pere Cheney is that it's in the middle of nowhere! Railroad tracks pass through the area where the town got supplies from many years ago before, there were cars and trucks. It's rather secluded and it is strange to see a cemetery in the middle of the woods. If I hadn't known it was there, and I had come across it by accident, it would have really spooked me!

If you want to find the old cemetery, don't rely on your GPS. It will take you down some nearly impassible forest roads. The best way to go is to take 4 Mile Road a few miles east of I-75 and head south down Beasley Avenue about a mile and a half. It will curve southeast into East Railroad Trail and follow along the railroad tracks. Travel about a mile and then there will be a road that crosses over the tracks. After crossing the tracks, turn left onto Center Plains Trail and about a half mile down will be the old cemetery. I recommend having an all-wheel drive vehicle as the roads are sandy and also get muddy when they are wet.

Trip Tip: The town once stood just north of where you cross the railroad tracks.

Point Betsie Lighthouse

Location: 3701 Point Betsie Road, Frankfort, MI 49635

Point Betsie Lighthouse is one of Michigan's more unique lighthouses with its white walls, green trim and bright red barn-style gambrel roof. Completed in 1858, the Point Betsie Lighthouse, north of Frankfort, is the oldest building in Benzie County. Standing along the shores of Lake Michigan, it marks the southern entrance to the Manitou Passage. In 1875 one of the first

83

life-saving stations was established by the U. S. Life Saving Service at the lighthouse. Many of the buildings around the lighthouse are now private cabins, but used to be part of the lifesaving station. It was built with Cream City Bricks whose pale yellow color blended in with the sand dunes. It was decided to paint the lighthouse with its iconic "Christmas"-colored paint scheme to serve as a landmark for passing ships during the daytime. Point Betsie was the last manned lighthouse on Lake Michigan, and the last Michigan lighthouse to lose its keeper after it was automated in 1982.

Erosion of the sandy point has always threatened the lighthouse, and in 1890 a ring of concrete was inserted under the tower. A curved break-wall was constructed at the water's edge to absorb the energy of the waves crashing into the shore. I think the blocks protruding from the surface of the concrete are there to keep the ice from Lake Michigan from pushing up to the lighthouse, but I could not find anything to confirm this.

If you want to visit the lighthouse you can find out more at their web page at http://www.pointbetsie.org/

Michi-fact:: The name Point Betsie originates from the Native American people who were in the area and communicating with the French at the time. The French "Pointe Aux Bec Scies" comes from the Indigenous word "Ug-Zig-A-Zee-Bee" which People of the Three Fires Tribal Council gave to a river flowing into Lake Michigan just a few miles to the south, where sawbill or merganser ducks thrived. Translated, Point Betsie means Saw Beak Point.

Trip Tip:: The lighthouse is a popular place for tourists but there is not a large parking lot for visitors. Most people parallel park on the street. If you have a travel trailer or motor-home it will be difficult to maneuver the small turnaround at the end of the street.

Gravity Defying Hill On Putney Road

Location: Putney road between Arcadia and Frankfort

In the northwest part of the Lower Peninsula is a road where gravity works in reverse. On Putney Road, in the southern part of Benzie County, strange things happen. This rural stretch of road is in the middle of the triangle formed by Arcadia, Frankfort and Thompsonville. Why does there always seem to be a triangle involved with unexplained phenomena?

The easiest way to find Putney Road is from M-22. About halfway between Arcadia and Frankfort, take County Road 602 also known as Joyfield Road to the East. About two miles down the road you will come to Blaine Christian Church on the corner of Joyfield and Putney Road. Take a right heading south on Putney Road. When you get to the curve in the road, turn around and head back north on Putney. Stop when you get to the yellow sign that shows a stop sign ahead. Leave your car running so the steering and brakes work then put your car in neutral and it will roll up the hill. As you can see it in the photo, the road goes upwards and only the top of the stop sign on Joyfield road is visible. I am not sure how to explain this, but it's the strangest feeling to roll uphill! If you do it, please be careful. It's not a busy road, but use common sense or maybe a bicycle.

Michi-fact: Another gravity hill can be found northeast of Rose City on Reasner Road. I also wrote about this hill in my first book, published in 2017.

Iargo Springs

Location: River Road Scenic Byway, Oscoda Township, MI 48750

Down the road from the Lumbermans Monument on the Au Sable river is Iargo Springs. There is a view of the river from the parking lot but to truly enjoy the beauty of the springs you need to climb down the 294 steps of the wooden stairway. Down at the bottom of the stairs, a boardwalk meanders through a forest of trees. Water rises up out of the ground and flows to the Au Sable River in a bubbling brook that winds its way around the trees.

The Native Americans believed the springs held mystical powers and it's believed that surveyors got the name for the spring from the local Indian tribes. The springs were used as a drinking water source and dams were constructed on the springs by early lumberjacks to divert water to the logging camps nearby.

Europeans have visited the springs for recreation since the 1920s. A trail to the springs was constructed by the Civilian Conservation Corps in 1934. The dams stood until 1981 when a storm took them out. The site was renovated in 1991 when the dams were rebuilt and stairs added, along with boardwalks leading to the springs. It is a beautiful site to visit. Well worth the effort of descending 294 steps and then climbing against the force of gravity to get back up.

Trip Tip: Be sure to visit Lumberman's Monument and Five Channels Dam, which is nearby.

Cross Village

Location:

6425 North Lake Shore Drive,
Cross Village, MI 49740

In a seemingly remote area of northwest Michigan, near the tip of the Lower Peninsula, on the shore of Lake Michigan is Cross Village. It is one of the oldest settlements in northern Michigan and for years the local Native American tribes would gather at this spot for tribal councils. Before he died in 1675, father Jacques Marquette erected a large white wooden cross on a bluff over looking Lake Michigan. It was this landmark visible from the lake, that gave the village its name. The small town grew because of the lumbering and fishing in the region, but it was Harbor Springs that became a popular location for many to live and Cross Village's population declined. Cross Village marks the northern end of the scenic Lakeshore Drive on M-119, which runs from Harbor Springs through Good Hart and the famous "Tunnel of Trees". Instead of Native Americans coming to Cross Village to meet in council it's tourists who come to the towns most famous destination: Legs Inn. Polish immigrant Stanley Smolak came to the United States in 1912 and settled in Cross Village in 1921. Using local timber and stone he constructed an inn and decorated the roof line with cast iron stove legs. That is how this unique-looking building got its name. Smolak continued working on his inn, decorating it with hand carved driftwood and tree limbs. He died in 1968 at the age of 81, but the inn he constructed still operates today, serving Polish and American cuisine to hungry travelers.

Michifact: A replica of the cross that Jacques Marquette built on the shore of Lake Michigan stands in Cross Village today.

Elowsky Mill

Location: 13796 Leer Road, Posen, MI 49776

Prussian immigrant Michael Elowsky fled the turmoil brewing in Eastern Europe in 1862. He settled in Detroit, was joined by his family, and migrated to Presque Isle County around 1870. Under President Lincoln's Homestead Act of 1865, he obtained his land on the north branch of the Thunder Bay River near Posen at no cost. He built a log dam and moved part of this structure from Trout River and eventually developed a complex of flour milling, shingle, siding, woodworking, and lathe operations. Residents of Metz, Posen, and Krakow Townships brought grain and timber to this mill. With the help of Thomas Edison, Michael's son Emil added a generator and electric lights to operate the mill 24 hours a day. The Mill closed at the end of the harvest season in October of 1963. During the winter of 1963-4, a great amount of snow fell, so with the spring melt, a powerful run-off on the river caused the original log dam to collapse. The great run-off also wiped out the saw mill that the family had across the river on the south bank. All the equipment was left intact and remains to this day. The mill sits on private property and is part of Hemlock Hills on Mill Pond. You can get a good view of the mill from the road.

Robert H. Manning Memorial Lighthouse

Location: In Village Park on Lake Michigan Drive, Empire, MI 49630

Lifelong Empire resident Robert H. Manning was born in 1927, and sold insurance for a living. He was an avid fisherman and took many trips on Lake Michigan. He loved to fish and would stay out after the sun had set and tell his friends and family how nice it would be for the town of Empire to have a lighthouse to guide people back to shore. After he died in 1989, his family and friends raised funds and built a lighthouse in his memory

94

near the boat launch at Empire Village Park. The lighthouse was illuminated in Manning's memory, and the Coast Guard recognizes it as a private aid to navigation. What could be a more wonderful way to remember a loved one, than building a lighthouse to have a light that shines in the darkness guiding others to safety.

Trip Tip: The remains of the Empire Lumber Company can also be seen at Empire Village Park.

Michi Fact: Lake Havasau in Arizona has 25 lighthouses that are replicas of lighthouses around the country. One of the replicas is of the Robert H. Manning memorial lighthouse.

Harriet Quimby

Location: Approx. 14500 Erdman Road 2 miles north of 13 Mile Road, Arcadia MI, 49613

Near the small town of Arcadia is an old farmhouse hidden in the trees behind a farm field. A baby girl named Harriet Quimby was born here in 1875, and lived with her family in this rural part of Michigan. When she was a teenager, she moved with her parents to California where she grew up and loved to write. She wrote seven screenplays directed by D.W. Griffith, and even acted in a few movies. She eventually moved to New York, and began writing a column for *Leslie's Illustrated Weekly*. She would publish articles about her journeys and adventures for the magazine, which lead her to an airshow. She fell in love with aviation, and became the first woman to receive a pilots license on August 1, 1911.

She became a world famous pilot, traveling the globe flying in her vibrant purple flying suit, and paved the way for female pilots like Amelia Earhart. She was the first woman Pilot to fly across the English Channel in 1912, but received little press coverage, because the *R.M.S Titanic* had sunk the day before her crossing.

On July 1st, 1912 she was tragically killed in a plane crash when her plane pitched upward, and she and her passenger were thrown from the plane and fell to their deaths. Strangely the plane glided back down, and her accident still remains a mystery as to what happened.

When looking at this old derelict house, it's hard to imagine the little girl that grew up in it, and the strong independent woman that she became.

Trip Tip: The house sits about 100 yards off the road in the trees. A Michigan historical marker sign next to the road marks its location. It sits on private property, and is not accessible to the public, but you can see it from the road.

Manton

Location: 202 Wall St
Manton, Michigan 49663

Back in the summer of 2013 I was staying in Cadillac and it was a cool rainy Michigan day. I decided to go for a drive, and I came across the charming little town of Manton. Near the center of town was an old mill with a sign reading "Help Save The Mill." I could tell it was an old mill because of the faded hand-painted mural on the side declaring it the Phelps Bros. Mill.

Also standing in the town of Manton is a Michigan Historical marker for the Battle Of Manton. When Wexford county was formed in 1869, the county seat was in the town of Sherman. A wooden courthouse was built in 1872 but the town of Cadillac wanted to be the county seat. After a few years of negotiations, the citizens of Wexford county agreed to make Manton the county seat. In 1882 an election was held and Cadillac won the vote but the citizens of Manton felt bamboozled because some of the the townships returns had not been counted, since the ballots had been mysteriously destroyed. The sheriff and twenty recently deputized men went to Manton at night to retrieve the county records. They snuck into town to get the records from the Manton Courthouse, but by the time they tried to take the three county safes, some of the residents woke up and chased the sheriff and his men away. When the sheriff got back to Cadillac, he raised a posse of a couple hundred men, a brass band, and a barrel of whiskey. They again took the train to Manton and encountered a hostile group of Manton citizens who were no match for the large drunken group of "Cadillackers", as they called them. The three safes were retrieved, and the county seat is still in Cadillac to this day.

It was the small town of Manton that inspired me to start exploring Michigan, to visit places that I had never been to see what is there. I would have never imagined my travels would lead me to writing a book: let alone two of them. If you are near Manton stop by to check out the nice little town and if you are ever near any small town in Michigan that you haven't visited, take a drive through town. You never know what you will find.

Metz Fire

Location: near 2046 Railroad Street, Posen, MI 49776

The railroad tracks that once passed through the little town of Metz are gone and are now part of the North Eastern State Trail for hikers and cyclists to travel from Alpena to Cheboygan. I wonder how many of those traveling the trail know of the devastating and tragic fire that terrorized the citizens of Metz.

It was a dry and windy autumn day on October 15, 1908 when a forest fire broke out near Millersberg. No one knows what started the fire but it spread quickly, heading east, destroying everything in its path. The town of Metz lay directly in its route. A train from the Detroit and Mackinac Railway tried to carry townspeople to safety. As people boarded the train, most of them women and children, some of the escaping people brought a few of their possessions, and loaded them onto the train, wasting precious time. The owner of the saloon loaded his bottles of alcohol to save them from perishing in the blaze. By the time the train left the Metz train depot, flames were surrounding the town. At Nowickis' Siding southeast of town cedar posts and railroad ties stacked up, burned on both of the tracks. The fire was so intense that it warped the rails, causing the train to derail. Twelve women and children riding in an open rail car tried to escape the blaze, but burned to death from the intense fire. Several others were severely burned. The raging forest fire burned a swath of trees thirty five miles long all the way to Lake Huron. As people began reading of the devastation from the fire in their daily newspapers, donations from all over Michigan began to arrive by train to the many people in northern Michigan left homeless by the fire. Women from the wealthy neighborhood of Grosse Pointe donated some of their evening wear. The surviving women of Metz wore some of these fine dresses, and they were probably the nicest articles of clothing the women had ever owned, living in rural northern Michigan. Everything in Metz was destroyed by the fire. Some of the buildings were rebuilt but the town was never the size it once was before that fateful day in October of 1908.

Trip Tip: A roadside park and pavilion with photos of the aftermath of the fire tell the story of that horrific day.

What Happened to Sister Janina?

Location: 6982 S Schomberg Rd, Cedar, MI 49621

In the Leelanau Peninsula is the small town of Isadore with a beautiful brick church at the top of the hill in the center of town. The current Holy Rosary Church replaced an old wooden church that held many untold secrets.

In the summer of 1906, Sister Janina came to the parish to help two other nuns in the school. A year later, in the summer of 1907, Sister Janina disappeared. After getting up early to do their chores, the nuns would take an afternoon nap and Sister Janina was seen closing the blinds in their second story dormitory. It was the last time anyone ever saw her. The other two nuns woke from their nap to find Sister Janina missing and the back door, which was usually locked, open. The community gathered together to search for the missing nun, but they could not find her. Nine days later, some residents claimed to hear singing from a nearby swamp at night, but were too scared to investigate. The next morning, footprints were found in the swamp, but it was not determined where they came from. For years the mystery of her disappearance was pondered. Some believed the parish priest, Father Andrew Bieniawski, had a love affair with her, but he was out of town the night she disappeared, and his alibi confirmed his innocence in her disappearance. The rectory's thirty-seven-year-old Polish-immigrant housekeeper Stanislawa Lipczynska became the prime suspect. It was believed that she murdered Sister Janina because she was jealous of an affair between the Sister and Father Bieniawski.

Sister Janina's body was discovered eleven years later when a new priest to the parish decided it was time to build a new church. He was told by some of the other local priests that he needed to take care of loose ends before he tore down the old church. After searching the basement, a skeleton was found in a shallow grave of the church. It was the remains of Sister Janina. Her body had obviously been moved there long after she disappeared, since it was not found in the initial search. The sheriff arrested Lipczynska and locked her up in the old Leelanau County Jail. The sheriff had a Polish speaking detective Mary Tylicka pose as an inmate to try to get her to confess. Lipczynska began to show signs of insanity so a psychiatrist in Ann Arbor examined her, and declared she was able stand trial. The prosecutor argued that Lipczynska was jealous of Sister Janina and killed her with a shovel, then buried her body in the church basement. The defense argued that the sheriff coerced a confession from her by torturing her, and leading her to a dark room with candles and a skull that had been manipulated to talk, scaring her into confessing to the murders. She was convicted of the murder and given a life sentence. She appealed to the Michigan Supreme Court but they upheld the decision. Seven years after her sentencing, Governor Alex J. Groesbeck pardoned her.

What happened to Sister Janina, and how her body ended up in the basement of the old church is a secret the building would not tell. Her death remains a mystery. Some say that someone confessed to the murder to one of the priests, but they would never tell anyone because of a Catholic's right to confidential confession. Her body was finally laid to rest in the cemetery next to the school where she taught so many years ago.

Sister Janina's story has been published in several books including *Isadore's Secret* by Mardi Link. A Broadway play was inspired by the tragedy and made into a movie in 1972, *The Runner Stumbles,* starring Dick Van Dyke.

Grand Traverse Lighthouse

Location: 15500 Lighthouse Point Road, Northport, MI 49670

As ships sailed past the treacherous Lake Michigan waters off the tip of the Leelanau Peninsula, it was evident that a lighthouse was needed to guide sailors safely around the point. A lighthouse was built in 1851 and its first keeper resigned after just one year. James Strang declared himself "King of the Mormons" and established a colony on Beaver Island, the largest island in Lake Michigan about twenty miles north of the Leelanau Peninsula. His followers would raid the lighthouse at night on a regular basis, taking fishing nets and supplies. The next keeper was Philo Beers, a Deputy United States Marshal. I assume he was assigned to the lighthouse to end the raids.

By 1858 it was evident to sailors that the light was built too far to the eastern side of the point. It worked well for guiding ships into Grand Traverse Bay, but was not much use in aiding the captains sailing on Lake Michigan. In 1858, the current two-story brick lighthouse was built. The old lighthouse was dismantled, and Philo Beers used some of the material to build a house in the nearby town of Northport.

In 1889, a brick building was constructed to house a steam whistle used to signal ships in the fog off the rocky waters at the point. It was powered by a steam boiler, and an assistant keeper was added to the lighthouse to help with running the fog signal. In one season the signal used forty-nine cords of wood. It must have been a lot of work cutting and splitting wood for the fog signal, and carrying oil to the lamp at night to keep the light shining brightly. By 1933, the fog signal was replaced with a diesel-powered air horn and in 1950, the light was illuminated with electricity. In 1972, a rather boring-looking skeletal tower was built off-shore and the electric light placed on top of it eliminated the need for the grand old two story lighthouse. The grounds were left abandoned and forgotten until 1984, when the Grand Traverse Lighthouse Museum organization took over the lighthouse and restored it. It now sits in the Leelanau State Park, and is open to visitors.

A volunteer keepers program allows people to stay overnight in the historic lighthouse. Volunteers say they have heard strange noises, such as footsteps on the hardwood floors when no one else is around. Some believe it is the spirit of Captain Peter Nelson, who was the lighthouse keeper from 1874 to 1890. After sailing the Great Lakes for many years, he settled down in Northport at the age of fifty five and married a Civil War widow who had two children. They also had three more children. Captain Nelson became the head keeper and he, along with his wife, raised their children in the lighthouse. Captain Nelson died two years after he finished his duties as head lighthouse keeper in 1890, and is buried in a cemetery in Northport. Maybe his ghost still roams the lighthouse that was his home for so many years?

Trip-Tip: Leelanau State Park has a campground so you can spend the night. It is a rustic campground without running water and only has pit toilets for a bathroom, however the location and view of the lake is worth the inconvenience.

Shay House

Located: 396 East Main Street, Harbor Springs, MI 49740

You may have seen an old locomotive on display in a park in downtown Cadillac. It was a revolutionary design patented in 1881, that had gear driven wheels which allowed for greater traction, kind of like a four-wheel drive truck. It was preferred by lumber companies because it could pull heavy loads up steel grades and around tight corners. Entrepreneur Ephraim Shay designed the locomotive for his lumbering company, and Lima Locomotive Works built and sold the engine licensed by Shay. Ephraim Shay and his family moved to Harbor Springs, and in 1891, he designed and built a hexagonal-shaped house with six wings opening off the central core, with a tower on top. The interior and exterior walls were stamped steel. Shay owned the Hemlock Central Railroad, which started in Harbor Springs. It ran about fifteen mile to the north and, of course, utilized Shay locomotives to pull the rail cars. He built the Harbor Springs Waterworks and later donated it to the city. His firm experimented with boats and automobiles, and in the winter he built sleds and gave them to the children of the town. It is said that he built over 400 sleds. He lived in Harbor Springs until his death in 1916. Shay must have been a remarkable person, giving back to his community with the money made from his inventions, while he continued to innovate. I wonder what he would have thought of Silicon Valley!

Trip Tip: In July, the Harbor Springs Historical Society celebrates Shay Days in honor of Ephraim Shay. His historic octagon house is open for tours.

Old Presque Isle Lighthouse

Location: 5295 East Grand Lake Road, Presque Isle, MI 49777

111

The Old Presque Isle lighthouse built in 1840, is one of the oldest lighthouses on the Great Lakes. It was not adequately built, and a second, taller lighthouse was built in 1870, on the north side of Presque Isle. If you are wondering, Presque Isle is a French term for "almost an island." If you have ever visited, you know exactly why it was given that name, since there is a small strip of land that connects the peninsula to the Mitten's index finger. Some say the old lighthouse is haunted.

George Parris and his wife moved into the keeper's cottage in the 1990s to run the museum and give tours. Sadly, George died at the lighthouse in 1992, and since his passing, the light mysteriously comes on at dusk and goes off at dawn, which is strange since the light is disabled. Michigan National Guard pilots have even reported seeing the light. After George's passing, a family with a young girl visited the lighthouse. While her family was in the museum she climbed the tower and when she came back down she told her parents she had been talking with a nice man at the top of the tower. No one else was around so she would have been the only one in the tower. She saw a photo of Mr. Parris hanging on the wall, and pointed to it and told her parents that was the man she had been talking to. Some visitors who climb to the top of the old tower have claimed to see a face staring back at them from inside the light fixture. George loved the lighthouse, and showing visitors around the grand old structure. He was also known to play pranks on the visitors, so now maybe he is playing one last prank from beyond the grave!

The two lighthouses are kind of "off the beaten path" from M-23, but it's well worth the trip to see the old and new lighthouse. Maybe you will see George illuminating the lighthouse at dusk.

P.S. If you are wondering why the light is on in my photo, I had a little fun with photoshop.

Lost In Michigan

Chapter 4
Upper Peninsula

Point Iroquois Lighthouse

Location: 12942 West Lakeshore Drive, Brimley, MI 49715

If you are heading up to Whitefish Point and Tahquamenon Falls, I recommend taking the trip from Brimley along West Lakeshore Drive that follows the Lake Superior shoreline. The road winds through the Hiawatha National Forest and inside its boundaries you will find the large Cape Cod style lighthouse.

116

When Congress approved the funding for the Soo Locks in 1853, they also set aside money for the construction of a lighthouse on Point Iroquois, to guide ships into the mouth of the St. Mary's River. The first lighthouse was built of stone and rubble, with a wooden lantern deck and stood only forty-five feet tall. About ten years after its construction, government inspectors began to question the integrity of the structure. In 1870, the first lighthouse was razed and a two-story lighthouse with a sixty-five foot tall tower was constructed. In 1905, an addition was added for another assistant keeper. A head lighthouse keeper and two assistants maintained the light and fog horn.

Point Iroquois and the lighthouse that stands on it mark the division line between Whitefish Bay and the western end of the St. Mary's River. The Point was named for the Iroquois warriors massacred there by the Ojibwe in 1662. Native Algonkians called the point "Nadouenigoning," composed of the words "Nadone" (Iroquois) and "Akron" (bone).

The station was deactivated in 1962, replaced by the Canadian operated Gros Cap Reefs Light, an unmanned buoy-type beacon in the St. Mary's River channel. In 1963, the original lens was sent to the Smithsonian Institution. Currently the lighthouse is a museum, and visitors can climb the stairs to the top of the tower. Although the light is gone, the view is spectacular.

The Stone Church On The Island

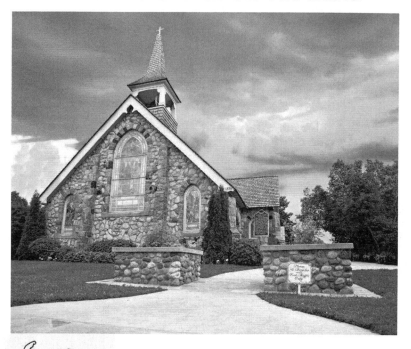

Location: 1590 Cadotte Avenue, Mackinac Island, MI 49757

If you have lived in Michigan for a while you have probably visited what Michiganders refer to as "The Island." I am referring to Mackinac Island. If you have toured the island, you have seen the Grand Hotel. You may have not stayed there, but most everyone walks up to its grand front porch. Cadette Avenue is the road that leads to the Grand Hotel, and along the way is a little stone church.

The Union Congregational Church was established in 1900, and local residents and summer visitors donated funds for its construction. The church was built using stones found around Mackinac Island, and the cornerstone was laid on August 2, 1904. The beautifully crafted stained-glass windows were installed in 1914, and tell the story of the Protestant movement on the Island. During the summer, the doors of the little church are sometimes left open for visitors to go inside to view the illuminated stained-glass windows. Next time you are on the island, and heading up to the Grand Hotel, be sure to stop by the little stone church.

Michi-fact: All fourteen windows of the church were made by the Lamb Studios in New Jersey, founded in 1857, and the oldest continuously operating stained-glass studio in the United States.

Manistique Water Tower

Location: 610 Intake Park, Manistique, MI 49854

Located along the shore of Lake Michigan on US-2, Manistique is an excellent place to stop for a break while out exploring the Upper Peninsula. You can relax at its waterfront park or take a stroll downtown. When you are in Manistique you may notice a strange-looking brick tower north of downtown. After running out of water to fight a fire in the early 1900s it was evident that the town's water system needed to be upgraded. A pumping station and water tower were constructed near the Manistique River. I am not sure why the community of Manistique chose to build the tower the way they did, but it is one of the most unique water towers in the country. An ornate Roman Revival style design was chosen to hold the two hundred thousand gallon tank. The tower was constructed in 1922 from bricks and a copper dome roof sits atop the 137-foot-tall tower. This unique tower provided water to the city until 1954, when the wooden pipes used to collect water from the river began to fail. A new system was built and the elaborate tower was no longer needed. It was used for offices until the Schoolcraft Historical Society obtained the historic tower. Along with other buildings on the property, the society runs it as a museum for visitors.

If you visit the tower you will travel over the world famous Siphon Bridge. I say "world famous" because the bridge was featured in *Ripley's Believe It Or Not,* as it was the only bridge in the world with the road deck lower than the water level of the river. The local paper mill needed more water so the level of the Manistique River was raised. The sides of the bridge are made of solid concrete, allowing the water level to rise up the sides of the bridge. The paper mill closed some time ago and the water level has been lowered to its normal level making the bridge just an ordinary river crossing.

Michi-fact: Manistique is referred to as the "Emerald City" for the greenish colored waters of the big spring Kitch-Iti-Kipi, which is a must-see if you are ever in the area.

Ford Sawmill

Location: 21235 Alberta Ave # 2, L'Anse, MI 49946

Henry Ford was obsessed with building the Model-T as efficient and inexpensive as possible. To do that, he used the process of vertical integration, Ford Motor Company created companies that supplied the factory with materials. Ford made their own steel, harvested rubber and built sawmills to supply lumber to the factory.

A few miles south of L'Anse on U.S. 41 is Alberta, where Henry Ford built a sawmill town in 1936 to supply lumber to his growing auto company. The town was named after the daughter of one of his executives. The community consisted of a sawmill, houses for the workers and their families, and two schools to educate the children while their parents were working.

Henry Ford saw all the sawdust that was created by his sawmills and felt it was going to waste. His sawmill in Kingsford, Michigan (named for Edward G. Kingsford who worked for Ford managing his lumbering operations) created an enormous amount of sawdust. A University of Oregon chemist, Orin Stafford invented a method for making pillow-shaped lumps of fuel from sawdust and called them charcoal briquettes. Thomas Edison designed the briquette factory that was built next to the sawmill and Edward G. Kingsford managed it. Ford sold the briquettes at his dealerships and after World War II, as the suburbs grew and the Webber grill became popular, the demand for the bags of black briquettes soared. Ford sold the company in 1951 and it was renamed Kingsford, in honor of Edward G. Kingsford.

In 1954 the town of Alberta was donated to Michigan Tech and is still used today for forestry education. If you're in the area, they give tours of the historic town and sawmill to visitors.

Crisp Point Lighthouse

Location: 1944 County Highway 412, Newberry, MI 49868

Note: Do not rely on your GPS to take you there. It will take you down roads that may be impassible.

Michigan has about 150 lighthouses on the shores of the Great Lakes. Some are easy to visit with a paved road that leads to a park where the beacon sits open to the public. Some are not so easy to visit, either being on an island, or out in a desolate part of Michigan. Crisp Point Lighthouse is the "other light" on the Upper Peninsula's Whitefish Point. The Whitefish Point Lighthouse, north of Paradise, is rather easy to get to, but the Crisp Point lighthouse is about twenty miles of dirt road through the dense Upper Peninsula forest. If you have ever run a 5K road race or maybe climbed Mt. Everest, you know, that just completing the feat is an accomplishment. It's kind of the same thing for the Crisp Point Lighthouse. Just getting to the lighthouse is an achievement.

The coastline of Lake Superior between Whitefish Point and Grand Marais has always been treacherous for passing ships. Sailors gave it the nickname "Shipwreck Coast" because of all the shipwrecks. The U.S. Lifesaving Service established a life saving station at the point in 1876, to rescue sailors caught in Mother Nature's fury. The second station keeper was Christopher Crisp and the point and lifesaving station were referred to as Crisp's point. Eventually it was just called Crisp Point. A decision was made that lighthouse was needed warn captains of the danger off Crisp Point, and to help them navigate the dangerous waters. In 1903, the lighthouse was built with an attached service room that still stands today. A two-story keeper's dwelling and a second assistant keeper's dwelling were built, along with a fog-signal building. An electric illuminated buoy was placed offshore notifying captains of the turn into Whitefish Bay. The lighthouse and lifesaving station were decommissioned and all the buildings were razed except the lighthouse tower.

In 1988, Don and Nellie Ross from Ohio found the abandoned lighthouse. They fell in love with the old tower so much that they moved to the Upper Peninsula and formed the Crisp Point Light Historical Society to save the remaining structure. Lake Superior eroded the shoreline to the edge of the abandoned lighthouse, and a storm in 1992 destroyed the service room, leaving only the foundation. The service room was reconstructed in 2006, and a visitors center was built in 2009. The society continues to maintain the lighthouse and welcomes visitors in the summer months.

The fun part is getting to the lighthouse. In the 1930s one of the men stationed at the lighthouse wrote in his journal that he traveled as far as he could by car and then hiked by snowshoe another twenty miles to the lighthouse. In the present day you don't have to hike, but it is a fun and challenging journey by car.

To get to the lighthouse go west past Tahquamenon State Park on M-123 then turn north on County Road 500 which isn't that bad of road for a dirt road, but then you get to County Road 412, which is a seasonal road, and that road is a winding, twisting path through the woods. The way to the lighthouse is marked with small wooden signs at the intersections. Also be aware that you will not have any cell phone service along the way, as you are in no-mans land in the Upper Peninsula.

When I visited in October of 2016, the road had standing water about every couple hundred yards, and you need to drive about seven miles down this road to the lighthouse. Thankfully I drive a Jeep, so it was not much of a problem for me, but I could see it being a problem for the average passenger car.

I was heading down the road, fording the water holes, getting deeper and deeper into the wilderness where cell service is non-existent. It left me without voice, text or internet on my phone out in the middle of Whitefish Point. I arrived at a spot in my journey where a sign on the side of the road marks the location where two sisters were stranded for thirteen days in their SUV, in April of 2015. I hoped I wouldn't have any breakdowns or anything. Signs are posted about every mile to let visitors know there is an emergency telephone at the lighthouse. The signs must have been added after the sisters got stranded.

After about twenty minutes of driving the seasonal road, I rounded a curve and there was Lake Superior and the top of the lighthouse peeking out over the trees! I got to the lighthouse and a couple came out to greet me saying "We were wondering if we were gonna get any visitors today." It was a husband and wife from Minnesota, that were volunteer light keepers for a few days, and they camped at the lighthouse welcoming visitors.

After taking some photos and visiting with the lighthouse keepers, I made the trek back to civilization. It took me an hour to get from the lighthouse to Tahquamenon Falls, but it was well worth the trip. If you have the time to do it, I would highly recommend it, but make sure you have a reliable car (or better yet, a truck or SUV) and you have plenty of gas. I burned about a quarter tank getting there and back, and I would also make sure to have some water and food, just in case.

Trip Tip: In the Upper Peninsula, be careful relying on your GPS. It considers seasonal two track forest roads as a perfectly normal route to take to your destination. This may be OK if you're a Yooper in a four-wheel drive truck and familiar with the area. Not so good if you are in a minivan with your family.

Sable Falls

Location: About one mile west of Grand Marais on Alger County Road H-58.

At the eastern end of Pictured Rocks National Lakeshore is Sable Falls. When visiting Pictured Rocks most people visit the western side and stay in Munising. It's kind of a long trip over to Sable Falls down the winding back road of H-58. Years ago this road used to be a rough dirt road, and few people mafe the trip. The road has been paved in recent years, making the trip much more enjoyable. Sable

129

Falls are beautiful secluded waterfalls, cascading down about seventy-five feet, flowing into Lake Superior. A wooden staircase with 169 steps leads down to the falls. Thankfully there are some resting places along the stairs, if you are like me, and need a break to rest your burning thighs and calves. The beauty of the falls through the dense green forest makes the trip down the stairs worth the effort. At the bottom of the stairs is a viewing platform where you can relax and enjoy watching and listening to the falls. Since it is somewhat out of the way, there are usually less tourists visiting it. The trail continues down to the mouth of the river where it empties into Lake Superior.

If you are traveling around the Upper Peninsula I recommend packing supplies for sandwiches so when you get hungry you can find a spot to have a picnic. Restaurants and stores can be few and far between so it may be a little out of the way to find somewhere to eat. If you do want to go to a bar or restaurant, Grand Marais is only about a mile away from Sable Falls, and has some nice places to grab a bite to eat, and some gas if you need it.

Michi-Fact: At the eastern end of the Pictured Rocks National Lakeshore is the Grand Sable Dunes, a five square mile area of sand dunes created by glacial actions. The French word "sable" translated into English is the word for sand.

Medical Miracle on Mackinac

Location: 7232 Market Street, Mackinac Island, MI 49757

Most people know Mackinac Island as a tourist destination. Before the fudge shops opened it was an important military fortification during the early years of our country. Many people don't know the strange story of how a unique medical condition, and a doctor on the island contributed to knowledge of the human body.

While at the American Fur Company Store on Mackinac Island, a young man by the name of Alexis St. Martin was accidentally shot in the stomach, at close range, by a shotgun loaded with buckshot. He was rushed to Dr. William Beaumont, an army doctor stationed at Fort Mackinac on the island. Dr. Beaumont did his best to treat the gunshot wounds, but expected St. Martin to die. Surprisingly, Alexis St. Martin survived his gunshot but after his wound healed he was left with a hole, or what is known by doctors as a "fistula," in his abdomen all the way through to his stomach. Because of his medical condition, it was difficult for him to find work so Dr. Beaumont hired him as a handyman.

Dr. Beaumont began performing experiments with St. Martin, dangling food on a string through the hole to his stomach. Every few hours he would remove the food on the string and note the digestion of it. The doctor also took samples of the acid in St. Martin's stomach to analyze it. In 1825 Dr. Beaumont was sent to Fort Niagara in New York and Alexis St. Martin went with him to continue the experiments. A few months later, St. Martin moved to Canada. After the experiments Beaumont determined that it was the acid in the stomach that digested food for nutrients, and not the chewing of food that was previously believed by the medical society.

In 1831, the two men met up again at Fort Crawford in Wisconsin, where Dr Beaumont studied the effects of temperature, exercise and emotions on the digestive system. Beaumont published a book detailing his experiments in 1833, titled *Experiments and Observations on the Gastric Juice, and the Physiology of Digestion.*

Michi-Fact: Alexis St. Martin lived to be 84 years old and fathered 17 children. I guess his wound did not injure his reproductive system.

Eagle Harbor Lighthouse

Location: 670 Lighthouse Road, Eagle Harbor, MI 49950

Many of the lighthouses that stand in Michigan on the Great Lakes are on a sandy shoreline. The Eagle Harbor Lighthouse however, sits atop a rocky harbor entrance, making for a picturesque scene popular with photographers and artists. Since the mid 1800s ships have sailed into Eagle Harbor in the Keweenaw Peninsula to seek refuge from Lake Superior storms. The first lighthouse, built in the 1850s, was a stone house with a wooden tower. It was evident that this was inadequate, and in the 1870s, the current red brick lighthouse was built. Ships' captains had difficulty spotting the lighthouse in the daytime, with the red brick blending into the surrounding natural rocks, so part of the lighthouse was painted white. Other houses and buildings were added to the lighthouse grounds for the assistant keepers and members of the U.S. Lifesaving Service. In 1962 the lighthouse was converted to an electric light. Because the lighthouse was automated it was determined that no one needed to be stationed at Eagle Harbor. The last person to live at the lighthouse was transferred to a different duty in 1982.

In the 1970s, a Coast Guardsman who was stationed at Eagle Harbor Lighthouse for three years told of his strange paranormal encounters. While living at the lighthouse during night, he heard what sounded like furniture being dragged across the floor of the second-story bedroom. The light switch on the main floor would mysteriously click on and off. He would see light coming from under the door on the main floor to the tower, but when he opened it, the light would disappear only to reappear when he closed it! On one occasion, a guest staying in the upstairs bedroom left in the morning frightened , claiming to have seen a ghost in a plaid shirt without a face.

The Coastie moved to the white house next to the lighthouse hoping it would be quieter. He said that house was even more haunted. While sleeping on the second floor he would hear footsteps downstairs that would go up the stairs, down the hall and stop at the door to his bedroom. He would be woken in the middle of the night by strange voices.

Stephen Cocking became the lighthouse keeper in 1877. He was born in England in 1836 and at the age of eleven he emigrated to the United States and came to work in the copper mines in the Keweenaw Peninsula. After serving in the Civil War in the twenty-third Michigan Volunteer Infantry Regiment he moved back to the Upper Peninsula. He was the keeper at Eagle Harbor until he died at the lighthouse of pneumonia in 1889. I wonder if he is the cantankerous spirit roaming the lighthouse?

The Coast Guard still operates and maintains the light in the tower but, the lighthouse is owned by the Keweenaw County Historical Society. It is open for tours from June to October.

Trip Tip: Out on the rocks in front of the lighthouse is a four-inch round brass survey marker.

Marquette Orphanage

Location: 600 Altamont Street, Marquette, MI 49855

If you are traveling down US-41 in Marquette toward Lake Superior, you will see a large brick building on a hill overlooking the road. The historic building, which has recently been converted into apartments, has been standing on the bluff for over a century and has a long story to tell.

It was built as the Holy Family Orphanage by the Catholic Church in 1915, and was designed to accommodate two hundred children. When you think of an orphanage you generally think of young children whose parents have died or abandoned them. There were some orphaned children living at the orphanage, but many were Native American children who were taken from their families in order to convert them to Christianity. In the late 1800s and early 1900s, white European Americans believed it would be best for the Native Americans to be assimilated into "American Society."

The orphanage had a dormitory, bathrooms, a kitchen and dining hall. The building also had classrooms to educate the children ranging from infants to 8th grade. The orphanage operated until 1965 and, before it closed, it cared for some Cuban refugee children. Operation Peter Pan was created by Father Bryan O. Walsh of the Catholic Welfare Bureau to extract children from the Castro controlled Cuba. Over 14,000 unaccompanied minors came to the United States, and the ones that lived in the Holy Family Orphanage were some of the last children to live there. Shortly after moving into the orphanage, they were moved to foster homes and the building was used as administrative offices. The building was totally abandoned in 1982.

Urban legends of abuse by the nuns, and a rumor of one girl who died at the orphanage gave rise to the building being haunted. The young girl was playing in the snow on a cold winter day. She caught pneumonia and died a few days later from her illness. Some said the nuns had a make-shift funeral for her in the basement. I am not sure how true the rumors are of the hauntings but the building has indeed been resurrected from the dead. The once dilapidated old building has now been turned into a beautiful apartment complex.

Alder Falls

Location: Near Big Bay off County Road 550 waypoint 46.78174N 87.7074W

I have been to a lot of different waterfalls in Michigan's Upper Peninsula, but my favorite is Alder Falls. Located northwest of Marquette, it can be a little tricky to find as it is on a two-track road, off County Road 550, near Big Bay. After parking near a little wooden sign for the falls, you need to hike down into a gorge to see the waterfalls. There are no steps, so it can be tricky to climb down and back up, especially for someone out of shape like me. I think that is why I like these falls so much; they are hard to access and find, usually there is not a large crowd of people. The times that I visited the falls, no one else was around and it was a peaceful place to relax and enjoy the waterfalls as the water rushed around the large rocks in the river.

Trip Tip: The falls are near the Big Bay Lighthouse and the Lumberjack Tavern that was made famous in the Jimmy Stewart movie *Anatomy of a Murder.*

Calumet Theatre

Location: 340 6th Street, Calumet, MI 49913

At the height of the copper mining boom during the early 1900s, in the Keweenaw Peninsula, the city of Calumet was one of the wealthiest cities in Michigan. To entertain the wealthy businessmen and hard-working miners the town built an elaborate theater. The city was one of only a few cities to have a government-built theater and it is the oldest continuously operating municipal theater in the country.

The theater opened on March 20, 1900. It had an electric chandelier made from copper to illuminate its ornately decorated interior. Some of the most popular and talented actors performed on its stage, including Douglas Fairbanks, Lon Chaney Sr. and the world-renowned Polish actress Helena Modjeska. Even the great Harry Houdini performed his magical escapes on its stage. The popularity of motion pictures replaced live performances in the 1920s. A projector room was built on the second balcony and a screen was added to the stage. For the 100th anniversary of the founding of Calumet, the auditorium in the theater was restored in 1975. The yellow and red bricks on the grand old theater were restored in 1988.

The building has been standing for a long time in Calumet and over the years it has seen many people come through its doors. It's believed that some of those people's spirits still remain. In the late 50s, during a performance of Shakespeare's *Taming of the Shrew,* actress Adysse Lane forgot her lines during a long soliloquy. She said she felt a strange force lifting her arm and pointing it towards the spotlight in the second balcony. That's where she saw the ghost of Helena Modjeska in the balcony mouthing the words to her. She was not the only one to see her. Many other patrons and employees have claimed to see Helena's ghost roaming the old theater. A portrait of Modjeska hangs on the wall in the historic theater and when it is removed from the wall strange things happen. The lights will flicker and not work properly. Strange banging and crashing sounds are heard, but when people go to see what has falen, nothing is out of place. If it is Helena's spirit, she found a beautiful place to spend eternity. The Upper Peninsula has always felt like heaven to me.

Legend has it that before the theater was built a young girl named Elanda Rowe was murdered where the theater now stands. Some people have heard a young girl crying and believe it is her. Others believe the cries are from young children are involved in the Italian Hall Disaster that happened on Christmas Eve in 1913. The miner's union was hosting a Christmas party on the second floor of the nearby Italian Hall when someone screamed out, "FIRE." During the panic people ran down the stairs to the exit. Many fell on the stairs, and were trampled and suffocated. Seventy-three people died, many of which were children. Their bodies were taken to the Calumet Theatre where a make-shift morgue was set up. Besides the spirits of children, the ghost of a man who was murdered in 1903 at the theater has been seen and heard. It's believed to be his voice that is heard screaming in the dead of night.

The historic theater is open for tours in the summer. If you are in the Keweenaw, remember to stop by for a visit. Who knows, you may be treated to a special performance by one of the ghosts?

Trip tip: The historic Red Jacket Firehouse is across the street from the theater and houses the Copper Country Firefighters History Museum. About a block away near the corner of Elm and 7th Streets, is the Italian Hall Disaster Memorial.

Lake of the Clouds

Location: The Porcupine Visitors Center is located at 33303 Headquarters Road, Ontonagon, MI 49953

If you have ever visited a natural wonder like the Grand Canyon or Niagara Falls you know that it's impossible to show the size and beauty in a photograph. The Lake of the

Clouds in the Porcupine Mountains is something you have to see with your own eyes in order to truly take in the beauty of it. The lake is located on the western side of the Upper Peninsula in the Porcupine Mountains Wilderness State Park. It lies in a valley and the Lake of the Clouds overlook provides a stunning view. A winding paved road leads to a parking lot, from there it's a short walk to the overlook. The park has over sixty thousand acres and 90 miles of trails to explore. The Lake of the Clouds should be on your bucket list. It is a place everyone should experience at least once in their lifetime.

Michifact: The North Country Trail passes through the park. It starts at Crown Point in eastern New York and ends at Lake Sakakawea State Park in central North Dakota.

Old Dickinson County Jail

Location: 705 South Stephenson Avenue, Iron Mountain, MI 49801

The last county to be organized in Michigan was Dickinson County in 1891. The county was named after Donald

Dickinson, a prominent official in the Democratic Party. He was a Detroit attorney and Postmaster General in the first administration of President Grover Cleveland. Shortly after the Upper Peninsula county was formed, a courthouse and jail were built near the Wisconsin border at Iron Mountain. The jail was built using red sandstone with a tower and a crenelated parapet roof line... in other words, a notched-out roof like you see on a castle. It was common practice in the United States in the late 1800s to construct jails and prisons to look like castles. Three of Michigan's largest iron mines were located in Iron Mountain. I am sure many hardworking miners have spent a night in "the castle" after an evening of heavy drinking.

Downtown Houghton

Location: Shelden Avenue, Houghton, MI 49931

It can be a long drive to reach the Upper Peninsula from the southern half of the Lower Peninsula. It's an especially long drive to the Keweenaw Peninsula in the northwestern part of the U.P. It was not until I was in my 40s that I made the trip over to Houghton. For years I would go to cities like Traverse City, Petoskey and Mackinaw City for weekend getaways. It was my trip to Houghton that made me realize how much of Michigan I was missing.

Houghton is full of wonderful shops and restaurants as well as a beautiful waterfront park overlooking the Keweenaw waterway and the lift bridge, which crosses over it. On the other side of the water is the town of Hancock and you can see the historic remains of the Quincy Smelting Works. The area is full of natural beauty and man-made historic landmarks. My trip to Houghton inspired me to seek out and explore places and towns I have not yet visited in Michigan. If you have not been to Houghton or the Keweenaw Peninsula, I hope you will make the trip to see what Michigan history and natural beauty you will find. I hope you will be inspired to explore someplace new in Michigan, and discover what you have been missing.

Bibliography

Hamburg

https://en.wikipedia.org/wiki/Hamburg_Township,_Michigan

Roming, Walter (1986) Michigan Place Names. Wayne State University Press

http://www.michmarkers.com

http://www.eststephens.org/

http://hamburg.mi.us/fire/history.html

8th Precinct Castle

http://detroit1701.org/EighthPrecinct.html

Eckert, K. B. (1993). Buildings of Michigan. New York: Oxford University Press.

https://en.wikipedia.org/wiki/Eighth_Precinct_Police_Station

https://usa.usembassy.de/etexts/his/e_prices1.htm

https://www.thedetroitlegacygroup.com/castlelofts

Engine House No. 5

http://fox17online.com/2014/05/13/allendales-engine-house-number-five-fire-museum/

http://www.enginehouse5.com/home

http://visitgrandhaven.com/listing/allendale-engine-house-no-5/

Kalamazoo Water Tower

http://www.kpl.gov/local-history/health/kph-water-tower.aspx

http://kalamazoostatehospital.posthaven.com/

http://www.kpl.gov/local-history/health/kph.aspx

http://www.michmarkers.com/startup.asp?startpage=S0244.htm

Huron Lightship

https://en.wikipedia.org/wiki/United_States_lightship_Huron_(LV-103)

https://www.phmuseum.org/huron-lightship/

http://www.michigan.gov/mshda/0,4641,7-141-54317_19320_61909_61927-54594--,00.html

http://lighthousefriends.com/light.asp?ID=166

Grand Trunk Railroad Depot Lansing

http://lansingcitypulse.com/article-8376-Depot-gets-new-shot-at-history.html

https://en.wikipedia.org/wiki/Grand_Trunk_Western_station_(Lansing)

http://www.michmarkers.com/startup.asp?startpage=L0521.htm

http://www.lbwl.com/Articles/BWL-Puts-the-Finishing-Touches-on-Historic-Depot/

http://www.gendisasters.com/michigan/16714/lansing-mi-train-wreck-depot-oct-1941

Bell Isle Aquarium

http://passagesnorth.com/2013/05/the-belle-isle-mermaid-and-the-rumrunner-by-mary-alice-rapas/

https://en.wikipedia.org/wiki/Belle_Isle_Aquarium

https://www.belleisleconservancy.org/

House Of David

https://en.wikipedia.org/wiki/House_of_David_(commune)

https://www.freep.com/story/news/columnists/john-carlisle/2016/11/13/house-of-david-benton-harbor/93069448/

http://www.israelitehouseofdavid.com/

http://www.maryscityofdavid.org/

St. Andrews Cathedral

https://en.wikipedia.org/wiki/Cathedral_of_Saint_Andrew_(Grand_Rapids,_Michigan)

https://cathedralofsaintandrew.org/about-us/cathedral-parish/cathedral-history

http://www.mlive.com/entertainment/grand-rapids/index.ssf/2015/05/cathedral_of_st_andrew_celebra.html

http://www.dioceseofgrandrapids.org/bishop/Pages/Cathedral_StAndrew.aspx#.WnSzTa6nGUl

History of Grand Rapids and Its Industries, Volume 1 By Dwight Goss 1906

https://en.wikipedia.org/wiki/Frederic_Baraga

Holmdene Estate

https://www.aquinas.edu/discover-aq/heritage-traditions/history

https://en.wikipedia.org/wiki/Aquinas_College_(Michigan)

http://www.therapidian.org/grand-rapids-historical-society-presents-quothaunted-holmdene-manor-and-history-aquinas-collegequot

http://www.mlive.com/news/grand-rapids/index.ssf/2011/09/aquinas_college_haunted_mansio.html

https://www.aquinas.edu/posts/history-brookby-estate-and-holmdene-manor

http://halfpuddinghalfsauce.blogspot.com/2015/06/holmdene-english-country-place-in.html

Castle Of Oz

https://castlepark.org/

http://www.dupontcastle.com/castles/castlepa.htm

http://www.hauntedhouses.com/states/mi/german_castle.htm

http://historygoesbump.blogspot.com/2017/01/hgb-ep-176-german-castle-at-castle-park.html

http://www.hollandsentinel.com/x586056714/L-Frank-Baum-and-the-Macatawa-Goose-Man-Celebrating-the-origins-of-The-Wizard-of-Oz

Peninsular Paper Co.

http://www.ypsilantihistoricalsociety.org/history/page996.html

http://www.nailhed.com/2014/05/embrace-your-citys-ruins.html

https://aadl.org/ypsigleanings/19529

Michigan War Dog Memorial

http://www.mwdm.org/

https://patch.com/michigan/farmington-mi/bp--guadalcanal-hero-buried-at-the-michigan-war-dog-m21b5b2008c

http://www.vdha.us/content20022.html

http://www.theoaklandpress.com/article/OP/20121109/NEWS/311099887

Minnie Quay

https://en.wikiped ia.org/wiki/Minnie_Quay

http://www.prairieghosts.com/minnie.html

http://michigansotherside.com/the-ghost-and-legend-of-minnie-quay/

https://www.findagrave.com/memorial/13580810/mary-jane-quay

http://99wfmk.com/minniequay/

Amos Gould House

http://owossohistory.org/amos-gould/

https://www.trover.com/d/Gq3a-the-amos-gould-house-owosso-michigan

https://www.geni.com/people/Amos-Gould/6000000000033743139

Roming, Walter (1986) Michigan Place Names. Wayne State University Press

Stepping Stone Falls

http://geneseecountyparks.org/explore/stepping-stone-falls-picnic-area/

http://www.mycitymag.com/secret-stepping-stone-falls/

https://en.wikipedia.org/wiki/Charles_Stewart_Mott

https://www.mott.org/about/history/

Linden Mills

https://www.tctimes.com/news/linden-mills-building-to-undergo-repairs/article_2ebf81f4-d746-11e5-ad0c-f707e788575c.html

http://www.michmarkers.com/default?page=L0160

https://www.shiawasseewatertrail.org/

Garfield Inn

https://thumbwind.com/2016/09/16/charles-learned-pioneer-builder-of-the-garfield-inn/

https://en.wikipedia.org/wiki/Charles_G._Learned_House

http://www.michmarkers.com/default?page=L0815

https://www.thegarfieldinn.com/

https://www.michigansthumb.com/news/article/New-owners-work-to-restore-Garfield-Inn-to-its-9197751.php

Lost In Michigan

Ammi Wright House

http://www.themorningsun.com/article/MS/20151214/NEWS/151219870

https://www.ourmidland.com/news/article/124-year-old-mansion-offers-peek-into-Alma-s-6970948.php

http://www.themorningsun.com/article/MS/20120521/LIFE01/120529978

https://en.wikipedia.org/wiki/Alma_College

http://www.northwood.edu/about

Wahjamega

https://en.wikipedia.org/wiki/Indianfields_Township,_Michigan

http://www.asylumprojects.org/index.php/Caro_State_Hospital

https://www.uvm.edu/~lkaelber/eugenics/MI/MI.html

https://www.tuscolatoday.com/index.php/2017/03/04/push-on-to-save-caro-center-2/

Roming, Walter (1986) Michigan Place Names. Wayne State University Press

Henry R. Pattengill

http://www.themorningsun.com/article/MS/20140814/NEWS/140819855

http://www.michmarkers.com/default?page=L2224

https://ca.billiongraves.com/grave/Henry-R-Pattengill/11356669#/

https://www.myheritage.com/names/henry_pattengill

https://quod.lib.umich.edu/b/bhlead/umich-bhl-852028?view=text

Roming, Walter (1986) Michigan Place Names. Wayne State University Press

Ovid's Gothic Church

http://www.ovidmi.org/history

http://www.ovidtwp.com/history.html

http://ovidhistoricalsociety.weebly.com/

http://www.michmarkers.com/default?page=L0114

Roming, Walter (1986) Michigan Place Names. Wayne State University Press

Omer's Masonic Lodge

http://www.mlive.com/news/bay-city/index.ssf/2017/02/local_history_buffs_renew_125-.html

http://www.michmarkers.com/default?page=L0444

http://www.us23heritageroute.org/arenac.asp?ait=av&aid=684

https://en.wikipedia.org/wiki/Second_Arenac_County_Courthouse

Port Hope Chimney

http://www.michmarkers.com/default?page=L0021

https://www.michigan.org/property/stafford-park-historical-chimney

http://porthopemich.com/index.php/history/

https://en.wikipedia.org/wiki/W._R._Stafford_Saw_Mill_Site

https://en.wikipedia.org/wiki/Port_Hope,_Michigan

Shepherd Train Depot

https://en.wikipedia.org/wiki/Shepherd,_Michigan

http://www.themorningsun.com/article/MS/20120226/LIFE01/302269971

Roming, Walter (1986) Michigan Place Names. Wayne State University Press

Croton Dam

https://en.wikipedia.org/wiki/Croton_Dam_(Michigan)

http://www.hauntedhovel.com/hauntedplacesinmichigan.html

http://99wfmk.com/crotondam/

http://www.michmarkers.com/default?page=S0684

https://en.wikipedia.org/wiki/New_Croton_Dam

White River Lighthouse

http://lighthousefriends.com/light.asp?ID=192

https://en.wikipedia.org/wiki/White_River_Light

https://www.michigan.org/blog/guest-blogger/the-keepers-behind-michigans-haunted-lighthouses

Oleszewski, W. (1998). Great Lakes lighthouses, American & Canadian: a comprehensive directory/guide to Great Lakes lighthouses, American & Canadian. Gwinn, MI: Avery Color Studios.

Saginaw's Castle

http://www.castlemuseum.org/about

https://en.wikipedia.org/wiki/Castle_Museum_(Saginaw,_Michigan)

The Beer Drinking Bear of Quanicassee

https://thumbwind.com/2018/01/13/jenny-quanicassees-beer-drinking-bear/

https://www.michigansthumb.com/news/article/The-bear-who-loved-her-beer-7308470.php

Roming, Walter (1986) Michigan Place Names. Wayne State University Press

Alabaster Loading Dock
https://en.wikipedia.org/wiki/Alabaster_Historic_District

https://michpics.wordpress.com/2012/07/28/gypsum-alabaster/

Roming, Walter (1986) Michigan Place Names. Wayne State University Press

http://www.ioscomuseum.net/history-of-alabaster.html

http://www.michmarkers.com/default?page=S0247

Pere Cheney

      Roming, Walter (1986) Michigan Place Names. Wayne State University Press
http://michigansotherside.com/witch-legend-pere-cheney-cemetery/

https://www.clickondetroit.com/features/michigans-most-haunted-the-witch-of-pere-cheney-cemetery

https://en.wikipedia.org/wiki/Pere_Cheney,_Michigan

Point Betsie Lighthouse

http://www.pointbetsie.org/history/

https://en.wikipedia.org/wiki/Point_Betsie_Light

http://lighthousefriends.com/light.asp?ID=199

http://www.terrypepper.com/lights/michigan/betsie/betsie.htm

Oleszewski, W. (1998). Great Lakes lighthouses, American & Canadian: a
comprehensive directory/guide to Great Lakes lighthouses, American & Canadian.
Gwinn, MI: Avery Color Studios.

Gravity Defying Hill On Putney Road

http://www.visitmanisteecounty.com/web-2-0-directory/gravity-

hill/http://michigansotherside.com/gravity-hills-in

-michigan/https://en.wikipedia.org/wiki/List_of_gravity_hills

Godfrey, Linda S., Mark Sceurman, and Mark Moran. Weird Michigan: Your Travel
Guide to Michigan's Local Legends and Best Kept Secrets. New York: Sterling, 2006.
Print.

Iargo Springs
https://www.michigan.org/property/iargo-springs-interpretive-site

https://www.fs.usda.gov/recarea/hmnf/recarea/?recid=18990

https://en.wikipedia.org/wiki/Iargo_Springs

Cross Village

Roming, Walter (1986) Michigan Place Names. Wayne State University Press

http://www.michmarkers.com/default?page=S0166

https://en.wikipedia.org/wiki/Cross_Village_Township,_Michigan

Elowsky Mill

https://www.hemlockhillsonmillpond.com/

http://www.us23heritageroute.org/alpena.asp?ait=av&aid=422

http://www.michmarkers.com/default?page=L2089

http://www.thealpenanews.com/news/local-news/2018/04/preserving-a-foundation-in-posen-history/

Robert H. Manning Memorial Lighthouse

http://lighthousefriends.com/light.asp?ID=200

https://www.us-lighthouses.com/robert-manning-memorial-ligthouse

https://en.wikipedia.org/wiki/Manning_Memorial_Light

http://lighthouse.boatnerd.com/gallery/michigan/manning.htm

Harriet Quimby

https://en.wikipedia.org/wiki/Harriet_Quimby

https://www.nationalaviation.org/our-enshrinees/quimby-harriet/

http://www.historynet.com/harriet-quimby-first-licensed-us-woman-pilot.htm

http://www.pbs.org/wgbh/nova/space/americas-first-lady-of-the-air.html

https://www.michmarkers.com/default?page=S0662

Manton

Roming, Walter (1986) *Michigan Place Names*. Wayne State University Press

http://www.michmarkers.com/default?page=L0079

https://en.wikipedia.org/wiki/Manton,_Michigan

https://en.wikipedia.org/wiki/Cadillac,_Michigan#Battle_of_Manton

Metz Fire

http://www.metzfire.com/THE%20FIRE.htm

http://99wfmk.com/metzfire/

https://en.wikipedia.org/wiki/Metz_Township,_Michigan

http://www.michmarkers.com/default?page=S0299

What Happened to Sister Janina?

https://mynorth.com/2001/03/traverse-classics-isadores-secret-of-the-missing-sister/

http://99wfmk.com/missingnun/

https://www.findagrave.com/memorial/153519887/mary-janina_(josephine)-mezek

https://www.atlasobscura.com/places/holy-rosary-catholic-church

Grand Traverse Lighthouse
Oleszewski, W. (1998). *Great Lakes lighthouses, American & Canadian: a comprehensive directory/guide to Great Lakes lighthouses, American & Canadian.* Gwinn, MI: Avery Color Studios.

http://lighthousefriends.com/light.asp?ID=711

https://en.wikipedia.org/wiki/Grand_Traverse_Light

https://mynorth.com/2016/10/ghost-at-the-northport-lighthouse/

http://leelanau.com/ghost-at-the-grand-traverse-lighthouse/

Shay House
https://en.wikipedia.org/wiki/Ephraim_Shay

https://www.shaylocomotives.com/shaypages/EphraimShay.htm

http://www.house-crazy.com/the-ephraim-shay-house/

https://www.michmarkers.com/default?page=S0248

Eckert, K. B. (1993). *Buildings of Michigan*. New York: Oxford University Press.

Old Presque Isle Lighthouse

Oleszewski, W. (1998). *Great Lakes lighthouses, American & Canadian: a comprehensive directory/guide to Great Lakes lighthouses, American & Canadian.* Gwinn, MI: Avery Color Studios.

https://en.wikipedia.org/wiki/Old_Presque_Isle_Light

http://lighthousefriends.com/light.asp?ID=180

http://99wfmk.com/presquehaunted/

http://www.angelsghosts.com/haunted_lighthouses_presque_isle_lighthouse

Point Iroquois Lighthouse

Oleszewski, W. (1998). *Great Lakes lighthouses, American & Canadian: a comprehensive directory/guide to Great Lakes lighthouses, American & Canadian.* Gwinn, MI: Avery Color Studios.

Roming, Walter (1986) *Michigan Place Names.* Wayne State University Press

https://www.fs.usda.gov/recarea/hiawatha/recarea/?recid=13342

http://lighthousefriends.com/light.asp?ID=566

https://en.wikipedia.org/wiki/Point_Iroquois_Light

The Stone Church On The Island

http://www.littlestonechurch.com/history.htm

http://www.mackinac-island-insider-tips.com/little-stone-church.html

http://www.michmarkers.com/default?page=L0644

Manistique Water Tower

https://cityofmanistique.org/manistique-water-tower/

http://www.manistique.org/oldtower

https://en.wikipedia.org/wiki/Manistique_Pumping_Station

Roming, Walter (1986) *Michigan Place Names.* Wayne State University Press

Ford Sawmill

https://www.mtu.edu/forest/fordcenter/visit/museum/

https://www.thehenryford.org/collections-and-research/digital-collections/expert-sets/101416/

http://www.lansetownship.org/township_history.html

https://www.michigan.org/property/alberta-village-museum

Crisp Point Lighthouse

http://crisppointlighthouse.org/crisp2.html

https://en.wikipedia.org/wiki/Crisp_Point_Light

http://lighthousefriends.com/light.asp?ID=722

https://trip101.com/article/crisp-point-on-lake-superior-a-bucket-list-michigan-light-tower

Sable Falls

https://www.nps.gov/piro/planyourvisit/waterfalls.htm

http://www.gowaterfalling.com/waterfalls/sable.shtml

https://en.wikipedia.org/wiki/Sable_Falls

Medical Miracle on Mackinac

https://www.michmarkers.com/default?page=S0019

https://en.wikipedia.org/wiki/William_Beaumont

https://mynorth.com/2017/05/the-gruesome-medical-breakthrough-of-dr-william-beaumont-on-mackinac-island/

https://www.mackinacparks.com/dr-william-beaumont-father-of-gastric-physiology/

Eagle Harbor Lighthouse

Oleszewski, W. (1998). *Great Lakes lighthouses, American & Canadian: a comprehensive directory/guide to Great Lakes lighthouses, American & Canadian.* Gwinn, MI: Avery Color Studios.

http://www.exploringthenorth.com/eagleharbor/eagleharbor.html

http://lighthousefriends.com/light.asp?ID=224

http://99wfmk.com/eagleharborhauntedlighthouse/

Marquette Orphanage

https://en.wikipedia.org/wiki/Holy_Family_Orphanage

https://www.clickondetroit.com/news/old-ghostly-northern-michigan-orphanage-being-turned-into-apartments

https://substreet.org/holy-family-orphanage/

https://en.wikipedia.org/wiki/Cultural_assimilation_of_Native_Americans

http://wondergressive.com/the-friends-of-the-indian-and-how-they-treated-their-friends/

Alder Falls

http://www.gowaterfalling.com/waterfalls/alder.shtml

https://livetheup.com/upper-peninsula-waterfalls/alder-falls#15/46.8258/-87.9912

https://www.travelmarquettemichigan.com/three-must-see-waterfalls-in-marquette-county/

Calumet Theatre

http://www.calumettheatre.com/about/

https://en.wikipedia.org/wiki/The_Calumet_Theatre

http://www.keweenawheritagesites.org/site-calumet_theatre.php

http://99wfmk.com/calumetoperahouse/

https://en.wikipedia.org/wiki/Italian_Hall_disaster

Lake of the Clouds

https://www.porcupineup.com/lake-of-the-clouds/

http://www.uptravel.com/member-110/lake-of-the-clouds-6470.html

https://en.wikipedia.org/wiki/Lake_of_the_Clouds

Old Dickinson County Jail

http://www.michmarkers.com/default?page=L0563

https://en.wikipedia.org/wiki/Dickinson_County_Courthouse_and_Jail

Roming, Walter (1986) *Michigan Place Names*. Wayne State University Press

Downtown Houghton

Roming, Walter (1986) *Michigan Place Names*. Wayne State University Press

https://en.wikipedia.org/wiki/Houghton,_Michigan

http://www.cityofhoughton.com/

http://www.exploringthenorth.com/houghton/index.html

I hope you will continue
to follow my journey at
www.LostInMichigan.net

Made in the USA
Middletown, DE
29 December 2020

30414355R00099